THROUGH *my* LAUGHTER *and* TEARS

Returning Home to the Bronx

A MEMOIR

ANNETTE STANZIONE

Through My Laughter and Tears:
Returning Home to the Bronx—A Memoir

Published by Wheatmark˚
2030 East Speedway Boulevard, Suite 106
Tucson, Arizona 85719 USA
www.wheatmark.com

ISBN: 978-1-62787-730-5 (paperback)
ISBN: 978-1-62787-731-2 (ebook)
LCCN: 2019907710

Bulk ordering discounts are available through Wheatmark, Inc.
For more information, email orders@wheatmark.com or
call 1-888-934-0888.

Acknowledgments

Putting this book together took a remarkable group effort from family, friends and acquaintances and I thank all of you from the bottom of my heart. Through all my heartache and tears, you have all been with me every step of the way.

First and foremost I thank God everyday for all the favor he grants upon my life and to my wonderful parents for making me the woman I am today.

An extra special thank you to my two wonderful daughters for believing in me and for encouraging me. My daughter Erica empowers women through her yoga training, spiritual guidance and retreats and my daughter Taylor empowers women through her fashion blogs, modeling and inspirational stories. I hope to do the same through this writing of my life experiences with relationships.

Throughout my daughters' childhoods they always heard me say, "I should write a book." They always knew how important this endeavor was for me.

I also want to thank so many of you for guiding and teaching me so much. I met so many fantastic professors, FBI agents, lawyers, authors, and co-workers.

Special thanks to my editor Tracy Quinn McLennan for

taking on this major task and guiding me in so many ways. Thank you to Wheatmark for the beautiful book cover design, layout and formatting of this book and for bringing my dream to a reality. The talent these people possess is remarkable.

The following has been inspired by real- life events that happened to me or as the accounts were told to me from others. All the character names appearing in this book are fictitious. Some of the details have been changed. Any resemblance to real persons, living or dead, is purely coincidental and should not be construed.

Contents

1.

Growing Up

I grew up in the 1960s and 1970s in a Catholic-Italian house-hold in the Throggs Neck section of the Bronx, New York. We had macaroni (not pasta) with gravy (not sauce), meatballs, sausage and, of course, plenty of bread every Sunday afternoon at 2:00, faithfully. We all talked with our hands, quite loudly, joining in on any conversation, at any given moment and knew what each other was talking about—an Italian gift. My grandparents always spoke in Italian when they didn't want us to understand their conversations. We kissed and hugged everyone that we greeted, hello and goodbye.

Forget about how long it took us to say hello and goodbye to everyone at a wedding or wake! Many years ago, Italian wakes could last three days with afternoon and night viewings. It was agonizing. Of course, everyone wore black.

I will never forget the huge Sunday dinners with the whole family and listening to countless tales from my grandparents about their childhoods. My family was very big on respect and manners. When you went to someone's house you never asked for anything and never went without bringing cakes, cookies or bread. Whenever someone came over, you emptied your cabinets to give them whatever they wanted to eat. We proudly upheld our Italian culture. Our weddings always played the Tarantella and we danced like lunatics. I can never forget about the Italian superstition malocchio, which is the curse or evil eye. Someone may give it to you if they were jealous or mad at you. The curse could have you suffer a severe migraine after it was cast upon you. A charm called the cornuto could protect you from the curse. When you wanted to sell a house you buried a small statue of Saint Joseph in the ground and ensured he was facing the house. My family believed death comes in three's. When someone died, you would wait to hear about the second death and then the third.

My parents grew up in Harlem. My Dad hung out at Thomas Jefferson Park. I was told in my Dad's younger years he was quite a gigolo. All that changed when my mom came along. On their first date my Mom had to take her sister to the movies with them. Oh yes, that would have really worked with my daughters! My Dad loved to hunt and mom loved to play bingo and they both love to go to restaurants and loved the casinos in Atlantic City. Maybe that's why their 64 years of marriage works so well. Back then when they said for richer or poorer, in sickness and in health, till death do us part, they meant it!

After they married, my parents were undecided about living in the Bronx or Long Island. My dad received a job offer in Brooklyn and the Bronx was closer for them to live, so we moved there. Dad worked three jobs at times, so my Mom could stay at home with my brother and I. My brother Joe and I went to St. Frances de Chantal, a Catholic school, which my parents insisted we attend. One day a nun smacked me across the face (something that is unheard of now) and I went home complaining to my mother about it and she smacked me, figuring I did something awful to deserve the first smack. Being a wiseass, I got caught chewing gum one day and had to walk around the whole day with the gum stuck to my forehead. The nuns were very strict and you always had to do as they said, whether you liked it or not. Ironically, I married in that church and now many years later I attend weekly mass in the same place I received my sacraments as a child.

My brother and I had a great childhood in the sixties, with a lot of friends on our block from Italian and Irish families. Every household had about four or five kids. There was always someone outside jumping rope or playing hopscotch. I was four years old when my brother was born. He was a cute little thing when I first laid eyes on him. He would go near the kitchen sink and I would tell my mother he wanted water. The king didn't even have to talk. He was the typical little annoyance, as brothers usually are. When he was little he enjoyed taking all the heads off of my dolls and wrote the word "YOU" on my Patti Playpal's forehead. Looking back, he probably could have written a lot worse. He had this thing about hiding stuff under my bed, like pot (when he got older). Was he hiding it for a friend, or was it his? My grandmother who lived downstairs at the time thought he had a gun under the bed. What a Commotion that was. We always got along fairly well and could talk about anything. He was like the sister I never had and he was quite comical.

I remember one day I had won Yankee tickets and wanted to take him and my dad to the game. My dad anticipated many people looking for spots to park, and asked, "Where are we going to park the car? My brother responded, "Where the other 50,000 people park their cars."

I was fortunate to spend my summers at the beach at my grandparents' house in Long Beach, New York. My mom didn't work and my dad would join us there on the weekends. My cousins would come some weekends and we would have so much fun. We rode our bikes everyday and were able to take a friend or two with us from the Bronx. It was beautiful there. We did see many accidents caused by the fireworks on the Fourth of July, however, and we also witnessed many people drowning on the beach, due to the horrible undertow in the month of August. There were many one and two family houses between the bay and the ocean. It had been forty years since the last really bad storm, until Hurricane Sandy hit in 2012 and pretty much devastated Long Beach again. My grandparents' house had beautiful mimosa trees with pink flowers. In the yard, there was a shower house to take the sand off from the beach. My grandmother hated the sand throughout the house. A neighbor who had four kids needed a mother's helper, so I would help her take them to the beach. I gave them lunch and snacks and watched them near the ocean.

Before the age of ten there is not much I remember, except having my tonsils out and ringing a bell so I didn't have to speak so Mom or Dad would bring Jell-O and ice to me and I spent a lot of time coloring, which I loved to do.

I remember wearing a training bra at ten. By the age of eleven or twelve my boobs were well trained and I wore a regular bra. This was a humorous memory of my younger years because my cousins teased me, saying "I probably could not see my feet."

There was a not-so-humorous, bad memory from the age of ten that I blocked out of my mind for many years, and never told anyone, until now. My grandmother and I were walking home from bingo which was about eight blocks from the house, like we always did. Three teenage boys walked passed us on my side and one guy grabbed my ass. They must have known what he was going to do, as they all walked away laughing. I was in shock and speechless, but, thank God I did not say anything out loud. My grandmother would have gone ballistic and they might have hurt us. I struggled with that horrible incident that happened to me for a long, long time. I thought if I didn't think about it, then it would go away when I got older and I would forget. But, that was not the case. I also struggled with the fact that I did not speak up for myself and I let them get away with it. Even if I told someone, I could not describe what they looked like. It was 11:00 at night and very dark out. As time went on I realized I did the right thing and hoped and prayed that they did not do this or anything worse to anyone else. I remember them bouncing a basketball as they walked passed us. I will never forget the sound of that ball. I consider myself lucky, considering all the sexual harassments and assaults that goes on in the world today. However, this was still very traumatizing for a ten-year-old child.

My first true friend entered my life at the age of seven years old. We waited at the bus stop together and were inseparable. We always slept at each other's houses. We walked and shopped at Westchester Square at Woolworth's and took the bus to Parkchester for more shopping. We attended all of our school functions together and later each other's weddings. One weekend, we decided to take an oldies cruise to nowhere around Manhattan. Johnny Maestro & the Brooklyn Bridge sang "Worst That Could Happen." We were the talk of the ship, with her name being Ynette, and, me being Annette. Whenever, we would introduce ourselves, everyone thought we were joking.

While I was growing up my mother made most decisions for me. She always suggested what I should wear, who I should be friends with and places I should and should not go. It pleased her. I figured she always knew better. If those decisions were wrong, it was not through any fault of mine. Later on in life, I let others make many of the decisions for me. It felt safe. It was what I was used to. However, some of the decisions made by others were detrimental to me and were certainly not in my best interest.

Speaking of pleasing others at our own expense, I have a friend who had a father who told him since he was little that he would never amount to anything. To this day, at the age of seventy, he is a workaholic, working from morning until night. He is extremely successful, but seems to still be trying to change the image his father had of him, even though his father passed away many years ago,

My parents were strict with me whether it was because I was the first child, the daughter, or because of the tragic murders by Son of Sam. At Catholic school we were required to wear uniforms that were gray and blue plaid. We used to roll up our skirts to shorten them and when I would come downstairs for breakfast, my mom would have me stop at the bottom of the steps, and with both hands, she would yank the skirt back down. When I wasn't wearing a uniform, I wore a lot of black clothes, as I heard my mom always say that black was slenderizing. She always loved black too. I used to go to the bus stop early on the corner to sneak and put makeup on. When I got older my mom would always say, "What time are you coming home?" and "Be home early." How could you be home early, when bands didn't start until 10:00 or 11:00 pm? She always worried so much.

I dated my first boyfriend from age fifteen to seventeen years old. My mom was very fond of him, and when we broke up she had diarrhea for a week. She was quite scared that now I would be going out with friends and did not have a boyfriend to worry about me and protect me.

My friends and I would hang out on the corners, drinking Heineken and smoking cigarettes to look cool. In the seventies the drinking age was eighteen. Until today, I cannot stand the taste of any beer. All was good, or so I thought, until one day my grandmother walked by and saw me and, of course, reported everything to my parents. I came home and my mother was crying and thanked me for the nice present. I asked "What present?" The next day was Mother's Day and she said finding out I smoked was a nice Mother's Day present for her. After having two children of my own, you have a greater respect for your parents and regret whatever you may have put them through.

One day, I was sitting in my business class in high school in St. Helena's Business School (the name was later changed to Monsignor Scanlon Business School), the teacher asked if anyone wanted an application to work for the FBI. After we all started to laugh, I raised my hand and took the application home. I recall it being many, many pages of information that they requested. While in Florida that summer with my grand-mother and cousin, my mom called and said I got the job, but needed to do some testing for three weeks. What the hell kind of testing took three weeks? I had to have my family's and friends' background checked. I needed to take a polygraph test and, of course, drug screening and another interview. And this was for a secretarial position—not a secret agent!

At seventeen, I started this job in Manhattan on 69th and 3rd Avenue, in the Hunter College building. I got all dolled up. When getting in the elevator I slipped in my platform heels (it was the seventies) and fell on the ground. Thank God no one was in the elevator. My arm hit the wall and my leg was under my butt. I was more concerned with making sure I didn't break a nail and made sure all ten were intact. Hey, I knew my priorities.

About a year and a half later I transferred to the FBI in New Rochelle, which was in the Sheraton Hotel, at that time. No one knew the FBI was there, of course. It was not something they announced on the outside of the building.

One day they had a tip that the Barclays Bank across the street was going to be robbed. We watched the FBI agents from our office circle the bank and the three men got out of the car with ski masks on and went into the bank with guns. The agents were in and out of the building and the gunmen came out with their hands in the air. It was like watching a movie—only live. The great thing about that job was, you could transfer anywhere, as long as they had a position open. One girl I worked with transferred to Alaska and never came back.

They say there are three men to every one woman in Alaska. Maybe that's why she stayed.

2.

The Early Dating Years

A *friend of mine at the office set me up on a blind date. She* told me that Troy had black hair, blue eyes and was tall with a medium build. She also told me Troy was a divorced country boy with grown children that he didn't see as they had never gotten along and he grew up on a farm. He spent most of his time growing up, tending to cows and chickens, and mowing his property, which had quite a few acres of land. I haven't seen many farms in my days, as I grew up in the Bronx which was mostly concrete without much grass anywhere. What would I have in common with a country boy? There was plenty of time for Troy to get groomed as the date was planned two weeks in advance, but apparently he decided to forego the whole grooming idea. Here was a guy who seemed to need a course in good hygiene. I, on the other hand, was raised to always try to look my best. I never left the house without makeup on. I always made sure that my clothes were clean and matched. Apparently, Troy was not raised the same way. It is funny when you try to picture what your date will look like and somebody totally different walks through the door.

When he arrived at the restaurant he looked like he had just plowed his farm. He also looked like he hadn't shaved in weeks. Go figure. I went on a date once and the guy asked me if I had shaved! Shaved what? My legs? My underarms? I know what he meant. Troy seemed to not really care about his appearance. He wore a plaid, flannel shirt, worn out jeans and black shoes and white socks (a fashion no-no, according to my friend). After talking for a while, it seemed that he wanted his girlfriend or wife to always care about her appearance to be sexy and to always turn him on. Troy had hair growing over his ears and he had more hair in his frigging ears than Lassie. My dog Oreo probably gets groomed more than Troy does. Maybe, that is why he could not hear me and kept saying "What? What did you say?" For Pete's sake, I felt like saying, deaf people can hear me because I am so loud. I have no inner voice. I didn't stick around long enough to find out if he ever changed his appearance.

Since my friend felt she failed me with Troy, she decided to try her matchmaking skills one more time with Brian. This guy's description of himself was tall, bald, with a few extra pounds. Okay, no problem there. We did not live very far from each other. We had a few phone conversations before we met, talking about the neighborhoods we lived in, our families and what we liked to do for fun. Brian told me the women he dated complained a lot about men sending pictures of their dicks, (his words). The words stuff, junk, private parts, and below the belt might have been a better choice than dick on a first date. Before the date he asked if we could change the meeting place, as his ex-girlfriend was working at the restaurant where we had planned to meet. I agreed.

When we met Brian put his cell phone on the bar and kept checking it. I wondered if he was he waiting for a call that he had to do surgery on someone, although I doubted it since he wasn't a doctor. I thought if he got a text, was that his exit out, if he didn't like the way the date was going? Who knows or cares, but it was very rude. He kept procrastinating about ordering dinner. Was he cheap? We ordered something light and began to talk. He spoke about his preference for certain sexual positions. Oh my God! Is there anything else you can think of talking about on the first date. I knew this would be the first and last. He told me two girls set him up. They were friends and he was dating them at the same time. What a guy. One day one girl called him for a booty call and he said his dick (again, his word) did the thinking, so he went. His private part came up in other subjects, but at that point I must have tuned him out and don't remember what he said. Unfortunately, sometimes I have a mouth like a truck driver, but there is a time and place to use it. I think a little more class would have been nice. Brian did not know me from a hole in the wall. I didn't care what made his private parts so great. The conversation should have waited until we knew each other better. Maybe, he was insecure about other parts of himself and his private part was what he chose to always focus on. Brian asked if I would go out with him again and before I could answer he said I didn't look like I wanted to. I guess my face said it all. He seemed surprised, like I should have performed cartwheels because he asked me to go out on another date. No thanks!

My friend gave it the old college try and tried for a third time. We agreed, "Three strikes, you're out."

Years ago there was a song called "Sweet Talking Guy," I think this guy gave the name to that song. I am sure this smooth operator always sweet-talked women to get what he wanted and needed from them. Sometimes, you may get really enthusiastic on a date. It's nice when you talk and have a lot in common and you get the feeling like you've known the person for years. It makes for a very comfortable evening. I would have liked to believe everything he told me, but, I was cautious. He was way too charming, too soon. You know that expression "too good to be true." Heed that warning. He said things like, "I broke the three-day call rule, but I had to speak to you." "You have beautiful eyes." "I love when you roll your eyes." "I knew I would ask you out on a second date after the first five minutes of being with you." "You are adorable." "We are both the same sign—it is an omen." "I love your accent." "Did I tell you how beautiful you are?" "Who does these nice things that you do?" and "When we're alone I want to do this and that to you." These compliments came at me like a herd of elephants. I didn't want to offend him, but I wanted to say, "Slow down! It's only the first date.

I should have noticed that while all these wonderful things were flowing out of his mouth, he was unable to look me in the eye. Sometimes we only see what we want to see. Was all this talk to get what he wanted from me? Did he finally stumble on a great girl—me? All through grade school I was called a motor mouth for talking so much, and I wondered how it happened that I could not get a word in edgewise with this guy. I didn't work fast enough for him and he never called again.

I really appreciated my friend trying to set me up three times, but, we both agreed she should not quit her day job and enter into the world of matchmaking.

~

As a mother, I can now understand the worry my own mother had for me, particularly in my teenage years. One of my best friends was killed by David Berkowitz, a twenty-four-year-old postal worker from Yonkers. His name makes me sick. I was at my desk at the FBI on a Monday morning when an FBI agent called me into his office. It seemed overly formal, as we always spoke together anywhere in the office. He asked me to close the door and when was the last time I saw my friend? It was only two weeks before that I was at her house. Her mom and dad went out, so she invited about ten of her closest friends and her brother for a dinner party. I still remember the white china plates and starting the meal off with prosciutto and melon.

Apparently, I had to be questioned, like all of her friends because they had no information as to who killed her. Killed her, he had said. I couldn't think of anyone on this earth who could possibly want to kill her. Those words rang over and over in my head. We were eighteen years old at the time and were very close. We met in high school and we used to stay at each other's houses quite a bit. She would give anyone the shirt off her back. I went home early that day from work completely devastated.

It was the first wake I had ever attended and I was hoping it would be my last. Not quite. Later in life, I would attend my grandfather's, two grandmothers', my mother-in-law, friend's parents, my uncle Louie's, and my fiancée (but more about him later).

As the story unfolded, my friend and another girlfriend went to the Peachtree disco in New Rochelle on Sunday night. It was around 1:10 am, in the Pelham Bay Park area of the Bronx, (ironically not far from where I live now) and they were in her friend's car talking. David Berkowitz came over to the car and he shot her and she died instantly and her friend was shot in the thigh and was in shock. Fortunately, her friend survived her injuries, but, she did not recognize the killer. He apparently just walked away.

Later, neighbors said they saw a strange yellow car in the area hours before the shooting. Before he was caught, in July of 1977, he killed six people and wounded seven others.

In August of 1977, he was indicted for eight shooting incidents and confessed to all of them. He has been in prison since his arrest and is serving six life sentences consecutively.

Many years later at St. Patrick's Cathedral in Manhattan, a special mass was held for couples celebrating their twenty-fifth and fiftieth anniversaries. While attending my parents' 50th anniversary mass, a woman came up to me and I thought I saw a ghost. It was the mother of my friend who had been killed. They looked so much alike and had the same mannerisms. Her parents were also there to celebrate their fiftieth anniversary. They had married the month after my parents. Her mom said my friend would have loved to be there and my parents were so lucky to have me witness their renewal of vows. Ironically, some movie scenes from the *Summer of Sam* were filmed in my family's neighborhood in 1999. I have never been able to bring myself to watch the movie.

After the Son of Sam horrors, I was very reluctant to go out at night by myself. I met this guy at a park, while on a morning run and agreed on a date. Garth was tall, dark and handsome and unfortunately not wrapped too tight. On our first date, we went out to dinner at a local restaurant. We talked a lot about a variety of things and I felt comfortable, like I knew him for years. (That's a good thing, right?) Something just wasn't right, but I could not put my finger on it. I accepted a second date to be sure I wasn't too fast in casting judgment over him. However, that first date should have been the last. He was craving a mudslide before dinner. While slurping away he had gotten the cream on his beard. I was a little embarrassed for him, as he was also speaking to the couple on the other side of us. I told him the cream was there and he wiped it off. A few minutes later it was there again, dripping down his beard. I told him again with the most finesse I could muster.

When it happened again, I could not stand it any longer. I said nothing. I couldn't care if it dripped to his feet. Do you not feel anything on beards or mustaches? I will never know the answer to that one. Thankfully, when he used the restroom he must have seen it and cleaned his beard. I was so happy to know the drink was finished and glad he did not order another.

After the dinner we decided to go to a nearby store. Garth had to get something for his motorcycle and I needed some cards. When in the automotive aisle he told me he was going to put the motorcycle part in a box that had a lower price tag. I told him to please steal on his own time and I will pray for him tomorrow morning at church and I walked away. That wasn't the worst part. When we got to the register I didn't realize this elderly couple was in front of me and I went ahead of them. The little old man said he was there before me. I said sorry, and I moved behind him. My date said that if he was not in a good mood that night he would have told the man off and knocked him to the ground right in front of his wife. Holy shit! This guy needed anger management and serious therapy! I guess his mom never taught him to respect his elders. What a great impression he made on the second date! Although he asked for a third date, it never happened.

3.

Marriage

I *met my ex-husband through a friend while in high school.* We dated for about a year and got married when I was twenty-one. Looking back, especially, compared to today, it was a very young age to marry. One night he picked me up for dinner and told me to get a CD in the glove compartment to play. I opened it and there was a small box, which was very nicely wrapped. He told me to take out the box and proposed to me in the car before we went to dinner. I was on a cloud. About six months later we married.

My mom had a great bridal shower for me, even though it rained like the monsoons all day. They say it is good luck, but, I laugh when I hear that. What else should they say—it's bad luck? Things were a little different back then. You didn't have to be tan before your wedding, send out save-the-date cards six months ahead of time and have bachelorette parties at South Beach or Las Vegas.

We had a nice wedding at The Astoria Manor in Queens

in December with about 140 people. While we were dancing our asses off, there was snow, sleet, and hail, coming down outside. After the wedding was over our best man and usher were in a terrible seven-car accident on the Koscuiuszko Bridge. That bridge was taken down and a new one was built in 2017. The accident landed my best man and usher in the hospital for whiplash and observation. Thank God they were released within a day. No one told us until after we got back from our honeymoon a week later.

We moved to Orange County, New York in March of 1981. I was very skeptical. I loved the Bronx and had lived there for twenty-one years. Due to good interest rates, we were able to afford a home in Orange County. What a culture shock and adjustment it was for me. I remember telling my mother it got so dark there and was so quiet.

When our daughters were born, my husband and I were fortunate to have both sets of grandparents always available to watch our girls, if we had something to do or someplace to go. Our parents lived in the Bronx, not far from each other. My husband did a lot of work on the house, adding a large patio and later, a pool. We had a bar in the basement and did a lot of entertaining, before our daughters came and took over the house. Our parents came for the weekends.

We had a very full social life. I remember fun Halloween parties with our friends, where we would all get dressed up. We loved to dance, so we would frequent bars that had music. He loved to ski with friends. I, however, was very happy on the bunny slope and then visiting the bar for a hot chocolate.

We played cards with friends in Queens from time to

time. New Years Eve was always a lot of fun. We would go with five or six couples to catering halls for the big night. Our town did a Fourth of July fireworks display around the pond from 9:00 to 10:00 at night. In the Bronx you would hear fireworks and ash cans going off all night. I was very surprised to find deer in my driveway and years later a bear on my lawn near my condo. The only times I had seen deer and bear was when I visited the Bronx Zoo.

I had been transferred to the FBI office at Stewart Airport. My husband worked for a gas utility company. He traveled quite a bit to Texas and Washington, D.C. for business purposes and we traveled a lot during our marriage with and without the children. After a business trip he would come home and I would need a break and literally ran out of the house to meet my girlfriends, like the house was on fire.

I decided to try my hand at gardening, since I lived in the country. I was a city girl who knew nothing about gardening. A co-worker had a farm with horses and she gave me horse manure for a great fertilizer. I would try to grow some tomatoes, zucchini and strawberries. I picked a handful of beefsteak tomatoes, as the rest were eaten up by worms. The zucchini grew to the size of baseball bats. They definitely did not have enough room to grow and the bugs got to the strawberries way before I ever did. Needless to say, the garden did not last very long. The worst part of it was the smell of horse manure that lasted for months in the trunk of my car.

I was glad I worked before I had my girls because I met nice friends, and we would go out a lot for dinner and movies.

I met a nice couple across the street who had not been married long. We became like Lucy and Ethel running in and out of each other's houses. We sold things at a local flea market with them to make extra money and we went to Atlantic City to see Frank Sinatra. One night, my friend called me to come over and asked if my husband could unload some shotguns her husband had. I thought, this is the quiet country I moved to? He was drunk and acting weird. We went over and later on we realized he had an issue with alcohol. After being married about three years, they divorced. A few years later she remarried, bought a big colonial house, had a beautiful daughter and is very happy with her new life.

My husband and I were married about five years before we had our girls who were born in 1981 and 1984.

I had morning sickness for a good seven months with my first daughter Erica. I labored for eighteen hours and looked like I got hit with a Mack truck. I had to have a C-section as she didn't want to come out. They gave me the drug Pitocin and I dilated from two centimeters to four. Needless to say, when they mentioned nursing her in the hospital I was not interested.

When Erica was two she was pretty quiet at one of her doctor's visits. The doctor detected a slight heart murmur. After testing at Westchester County Medical Center the doctors found a pin size hole in her heart. It didn't affect her breathing. They said if the hole didn't close on its own by the time she was five, she would need it to be surgically closed. My husband and I traveled to Westchester Country Medical Center every November for the next three years and luckily it closed on its own. I will never forget how scary that was. Through her childhood Erica needed braces, contacts and surgery for a deviated septum.

$$\sim$$

Four years later I became pregnant with Taylor. I did not have morning sickness, but, had headaches for three or four months. Since my pelvic bone was small, which was the reason I never dilated with Erica, Taylor was a planned C-section and was born at 8:00 am.

I tried to earn extra money while staying home and watched a little girl Erica's age for two years. Toilet training was pretty easy because they mimicked each other. When they were four years old, I had my second daughter and had to stop babysitting her. It would have been too much for me to babysit for two four years olds and an infant every day. Erica did not sleep a full, straight night until she was two years old. My mother said once she got christened, God will have her and she will sleep, but that didn't work. Then my mother said when she went on solid foods she would then sleep the night. That didn't work either. So when Taylor came along I was afraid I'd be in for the same sleeping schedule. But Taylor was a much better sleeper—thank God.

My girls loved living in Monroe and had many friends. Fortunately, I was able to stay at home with them when they were small. I helped out in the school kitchen for the healthy eating fairs, cutting up pounds and pounds of fruit and veggies. I was the Kool-Aid mom too, and was always in the driveway handing out snacks. I remember feeling better knowing my girls were safe in front of my house.

~

There were funny memories of raising my daughter. At my daughter Erica's third birthday party as a local pizzeria I guess she was tired of playing Pin the Tail on the Donkey and yelled out, "I don't want to play this fucking game anymore!" My mom and the other mothers were there as well. I thought I would faint.

My friend and I started designing clothing for women for some extra money. We had house parties and rented out church basements. We called ourselves A & A Designs. Her name started with the same letter as mine.

We would go into Manhattan to buy T-shirts and pant sets and we also sold earrings, belts, and handbags. After a day in the city having lunch and buying things for ourselves, I have to wonder how prosperous this venture was. It did, however, keep us busy, and we had spare money to buy frivolous things.

My husband and I traveled quite a bit alone, with friends and with our daughters. Italy was my favorite destination when I was single, but Hawaii was also a great place, where my husband and I vacationed. I remember having fun shopping for the girls and bringing home little grass hula skirts for them. While having loads of fun in Hawaii, my mom was in the Bronx watching my two girls, Erica age six and Taylor, age two and she was not having as much fun. Erica came down with an ear infection, screaming until my friend got antibiotics for her. Taylor's godmother came to get Taylor for a few hours to give my mom a break and the screaming started all over again because Erica did not go too. My mother wanted to kiss the ground when we arrived back and anytime Hawaii is mentioned my mom cringes.

For the most part, as the girls got older they got along well, but, one day I came home to hear cursing and bloodcurdling screams. One had taken the other one's sweater without asking and they were each tugging on a sleeve. I felt like taking a scissor and cutting the sweater right up the middle. I thought the earlier childhood years were difficult, but I never imagined what the teenage years would be like.

One day a neighbor called and said she didn't know Erica got her license. Laughing, I said, "Wow, I didn't know that either!" When I was at work Erica was driving my car all around the development—without her license. I don't miss those teenage years. Daughters!

They both played soccer when they were young and they had developed a great love of yoga, fashion and traveling. In this high-energy and competitive world we live in, I'm glad that they have yoga to de-stress. We also love to run. When they saw me and I looked stressed out they would tell me to go for a run to clear my head.

Erica went on to attend a college on Long Island. After dropping her and her stuff off, I gave her an emergency charge card with a $500 limit just in case we forgot a book or some toiletries. The first month's bill arrived for $500, for what my daughter thought, were emergencies. She had purchased clothes, tanning sessions, concert tickets, train tickets to the city—even a $6 piece of cheesecake from a restaurant! I blew a fuse. She worked part-time while in college and paid that bill. I guess I should have explained better what emergencies were.

I was very focused on being a good wife and mother, having dinner on the table every night and having my girls enrolled in many social activities. Having my girls was the most fulfilling part of my life. I raised my daughters to spread their wings and be whatever they want to be. I would always be their biggest fan. I took Erica's yoga classes and retreats, even though I do the worse downward dog pose due to my weak wrists. When Taylor started her fashion blog I sent it to everyone that I know.

If I could give my daughters three things, it would be the wisdom to know their self-worth, the strength to chase their dreams and the ability to say no to anything in their life that does not bring them happiness!

4.

Single Motherhood

*M*y husband and I somehow started to drift apart. Going through my divorce was horrible, especially with having two children to worry about. At the time, I didn't know anyone who was divorced. I had so many unanswered questions. I never had a plan B and believed in "till death do us part." When you are divorced, I think you try even harder to get everything right. I probably did a lot of things wrong in life, but I definitely got it right with my daughters. I made sure I raised them to always have plan B to fall back on. When I grew up, everyone was getting married, having babies and living happily ever after. I grew up believing things are black or white with no shaded gray areas. But as my therapist would say, thinking and believing this leads to a very limited vision in life.

At my first therapy visit, I sat on the couch and guessed he sensed I was sad when he handed me a box of tissues. I said, *oh, no thank you, I am fine.* It didn't take me too long to go through half a box of tissues. He knew his patients. I would go to his home office for appointments and had phone conversations when he was pressed for time. He is a wonderful psychotherapist—not psychiatrist, so he couldn't administer drugs—which was probably a good thing. I have recommended him many times to others.

I did not want the girls going through a divorce and having their house sold, so I tried my best to keep everything stable for nine years, before selling and moving into a condo. I could not afford to hire people, so the pool, mowing, shoveling, painting, wallpapering and even blacktopping the driveway became my responsibility.

My part time job had to turn full time, due to financial reasons and I needed to get my own medical plan. The girls were old enough to stay home alone while I worked.

No matter how many years you spend in therapy, therapists always have a way of putting things in perspective, particularly with many things you knew before you walked into the office. My therapist once asked me what I liked to do. I was speechless. I had spent so much time taking care of my kids, the house and my marriage, that I had no idea who I was anymore other than what I was to others.

He has helped me immensely through the years with my relationships, advice about real estate when selling my condo, but most of all working on myself. He said many things, but one that always stuck in my head was: "You have to know where you came from before you know where you are going." I took that to mean you have to let things in the past go before you can truly move on. When I mentioned to my parents I was seeing a therapist, my mom asked if the people in the country are crazy. I don't think they could fathom why I would need to speak to a stranger about personal issues. Back in their day if you saw a therapist you were probably living in a mental facility. I tried to explain you go to a foot doctor for your feet, bone doctor, etc. We never did have that conversation again.

What a beautiful thing it is, to be able to stand tall and say, "I fell apart, and I survived."

As I said, I kept the house for nine years—mowing, shoveling, taking care of the pool and resurfacing the driveway with tar. I actually had special sneakers, brooms and stuff to do that task. I refinanced the house and sat in the closing just signing my name away, hoping I was being led in the right direction with the attorneys, realtors and my buyer.

It was now my time to be able to care for myself like I should and pursue my passions.

One of my passions was singing. I had a few lessons in high school and actually sang "Killing Me Softly" solo. Boy, did I have nerve to attempt that song! When my children were small I joined my church choir at Sacred Heart and sang my little heart out for many years. My choir director gave me lessons in exchange for me taking care of her cats when she was away. Although I don't read music, she said I had a good ear. I tried to follow the likes of Barbara Streisand, Jennifer Lopez, Diana Ross, and Jennifer Hudson. Of course, I sounded nothing like any of them.

You know you are very passionate about something when you do it and it puts you in another world, something like an outer body experience. I was told I was a soprano, and behind me in the choir were the mezzo sopranos. While trying to reach the notes with them one Sunday, I almost passed out.

I used to write poems when I was in grammar school. I was more interested in writing stories. One day I sat down to write (before computers) and, when I looked at the clock, four hours had passed. That's when I knew writing was also a passion of mine. I consider myself lucky. I think some people go through life never knowing what their passions are and, if they do know, they may never pursue them for one reason or another. Although, I am not a saver of many things, I've always saved what I wrote. I filled up diaries very fast when I was young. It was quite normal for me to read two or three books at the same time—my favorites were autobiographies.

I have a friend who lives in Versailles, Kentucky, with whom I worked many years ago in the FBI. We have been writing to each other the old-fashioned way by sending letters in the mail every two or three weeks for about thirty something years now. It's funny in this day and age with computers and so many ways to stay in touch with people that we still write letters with nice stationery.

After my divorce I worked in retail at one of the biggest tourist attractions in New York, Woodbury Commons. I had a weekday off and the girls and I were planning on swimming in our pool the next day. The night before, I cleaned the pool and we all went to bed. On occasion there would be a dead squirrel in the pool or a chipmunk that perhaps fell out of the tree and I would have to ask a neighbor to skim out these little creatures.

I certainly couldn't do it. I had never seen what I

encountered the next morning. I got up early and while the girls were still sleeping I went to admire how nice the pool looked, but I saw that the water was brown and red. I nearly had a heart attack. At the bottom of the pool was a large dog. I did not want the girls to wake up and see it. I called the police and my best friend, a vet and the ASPCA. My friend arrived first for my moral support, smoking one cigarette after the other. She was a nervous wreck. The police then came and asked if I knew anyone who would do this? Were they kidding? I gave them a huge garbage bag and they had a rod with a hook to haul the dog out. The collar had no identification—just pink pigs. It was a beautiful yellow lab. We think the dog ate poison somewhere and went into the pool to drink the water. I asked the vet and ASPCA if the dog had a disease could we catch it and they answered "no," but, suggested I drain the water out, add new water and shock the shit out of it. When all was done, I used the pool first and after I didn't get any sores, infections or died, I let the kids swim again. Who does this shit happen too? *Me!*

I had to get out of retail as the nights and weekends were a killer. I loved secretarial at the FBI and wanted to get back into a nine-to-five job. I applied for a secretarial/legal position in Rockland County and got the job. I met such wonderful ladies there and we are all still friends today. The first day I was there, the attorney I worked for asked me what court he was going to that day as I was in charge of his calendar. I told him, "Westchesta Courthouse." He asked where and again I said "Westchesta." When he asked a third time I said louder "Westchesta" and under my breath, I said *"Does he have a hearing problem?"* I didn't remember him having a hard time hearing me at the interview. Anyway, he finally said "Annette it is WestchestER." I knew he could take a joke, so I told him where I come from it is "motha, fatha, Westchesta." You can take the girl out of the Bronx, but you can't take the Bronx out of the girl.

While working in the legal field, I met many men.

Fred did not have a photo posted on the dating website, which everyone should be wary of. It either means they are married or, in this case, a professional that is very guarded about his personal life. We had a nice conversation and then he texted me a photo. Don't get me wrong I am a very affectionate and attentive person, but Fred was all over me on the first date in the frigging restaurant. Mind you, there was a couple at the next table who he introduced me to before we sat down for dinner. Maybe he was showing off that he was with me (Show some restraint, I know I'm hot, ha ha). I'm not sure if he was showing off or I was just so irresistible? How many years had it been since his last date? He moved his chair close to me before the food arrived and asked if I had a problem showing my affection in public (while trying to make out with me, does a good kiss get you a second date?). I said I had no problem showing affection in public. What I should have said is that I would show my affection to someone at Yankee Stadium, the beach, anywhere, if I knew them longer than an hour. I'm glad he moved over when the food arrived and he didn't suggest me feeding him.

The second date pretty much went the same way. We walked outside by the river holding hands. We ate at an outside restaurant and, again, he practically sat on my lap. If you talk enough, you find out a lot about people. Fred wanted the storybook romance with all the love that goes on forever. I think a lot of us want that. He said he would have liked it if any of his ex-girlfriends left a toothbrush or some clothes at his house when they stayed over. What difference did it make if she leaves a little overnight bag or took her stuff back and forth from her house to his? He was a nice guy, but, too needy.

I later found out from mutual friends that he had a new girlfriend every month and he gave the last girlfriend, who would not leave a toothbrush at his house, a big expensive birthday party with a beautiful heartfelt speech and then she left him. So sad.

When I was a kid, I remember you knew a boy liked you because he pulled your hair in the school hallway, pushed you gently, teased you or blew spitballs at you through a straw. Ah, things were so simple then. These days no one can seem to figure anything out. I remember running into a woman I had not seen for a long time and I asked her if she was dating. She said, "What is a date? Like a fig, a fruit?" I guess her dance card was blank for quite some time.

A man named Kurt showed me that he really liked me. He was a DJ at a singles dance. I was on the dance floor and he started to dance with me. Kurt was quite the dancer, probably because he has music in his head all the time as a DJ. We danced all night, but he told me he lived far away in New Jersey and came with a bunch of guys. Kurt wanted to see me the following Saturday night, but he had to DJ a good friend's wedding. He said they would not mind if I came. I could meet him there, help him DJ, eat great food and dance my ass off. I said why not, and Kurt could play my favorites songs. I met him at the catering hall and went behind the DJ table with him. There must have been about 250 people at this wedding. I took requests from some of the guests and we played them. I was a little nervous, but after a little while, I was pulling people out of their seats, passing out party hats, sunglasses and leis and leading the frigging conga line all around the dance floor. I was so in my element. They must have thought I had been doing this for years. At the end of the night he made an announcement that he did the wedding music for free and he tore up the bride and groom's contract. What a sweet guy. Everyone applauded.

While putting all the music away he told me he lost his job a while back and lived with an aunt. He had sold his car for some money, but he wasn't able to drive anyway, as he had gotten a DWI recently. He started the DJ business to make some money. He couldn't afford to go out, but said maybe in the future when he got on his feet we could get together again. It must have taken a lot to tell me that. I thanked him for his honesty. I felt so bad for him. Playing DJ for the evening made it one of the best dates I ever had. I never did hear from him.

I think I could say I have had my share of the disco dancers.

Ben and I met at a singles dance, and Ben was quite a dancer. He had taken lessons many years ago at the insistence of an ex-girlfriend. I felt like I was dating Fred Astaire. Ben and I danced everywhere. Don't get me wrong, I love to dance also. The hustle was his dance of choice. He came at me like a bat out of hell. Ben was a carpenter all of his life, so, when I moved into my condo he was a tremendous help with the moving, painting, and more.

One night we went to a Halloween party at his friend's house. It seemed that everyone knew each other. They played a game that was similar to musical chairs. When the music stopped you had to sit on someone's lap and try to break a balloon. I was trying to fit in and have his friends like me. I thought the game was silly, but fun. Without making much of an effort I had everyone laughing, everyone except Ben. He gave me a sullen look and an attitude. I was just being myself. Was he worried that I was the center of attention for ten frigging minutes? Afterward we had a tremendous fight. He said I got along a little too well with his friends. In the meantime, they were all with girlfriends and wives and everyone seemed to be enjoying themselves. It was all so uncalled for. I realized something was not right, aside from him being very jealous. I never gave him any reason to distrust me, so I believe his trust issues were stemming from his relationships many years prior. I always second-guessed myself because he was so insanely jealous. Looking back and remembering him speak about his childhood, I should have taken notes, because he dealt with a lot of demons throughout his childhood, which, I found out later could be a symptom of a psychological problem. He had feelings of inadequacy and insecurity, and became overly dependent on others. These kind of people tend to be more jealous than others.

He always said he could not believe he met someone like

me and what did he do to deserve me. I could never believe how a stupid game at a Halloween party could make such an impact on our relationship that barely lasted a year.

It was strange how he could look so normal on the outside. I went on a job estimate with him once to have a bathroom redone and the couple was trying to chew him down on the price a little (as we all have done), but he got into a fit of rage and walked out. Ben turned down other jobs after that because they were menial jobs. Did he think he was a prima Donna? A long time ago, I had a full-time job during the week and a part-time one on the weekends. You do what you have to do. I wanted to say, for Pete's sake, have some respect for yourself and, take anything that will pay the bills. Financially, he really could not afford to let any work slip out of his hands.

As time went on he seemed to suffer from depression and later threatened suicide. He spoke a lot about all of the discouragements in his life and always saw himself as a victim. Talking to him on the phone made me either want to shoot him through the phone or shoot myself when I got off the phone. He was very toxic. Did anyone in his life ever love, help or understand him? I had a boyfriend when I was a teenager who also threatened suicide when I broke up with him. I guess he eventually got over me because he is still alive today and married with children, thank God. I knew it was time to move on. As much as I try to help people, I know that some things are not in my control. No matter how hard I would try to lift him up, he would drag me down. Looking back, I could see the scenario, if I stayed. I might have tried to get him into therapy—something he said he had tried a long time ago. I could have dated him until he sucked all of the emotional life out of me. I could have watched him sitting on the couch watching TV. Lastly, I could have hoped and prayed that someday he would get well. I chose to leave.

Looking back, I realized what a great waste of time and breath I spent trying to reason with someone who could never understand reasoning. He did try to tell me, inadvertently about his less-than-happy childhood followed by his poor relationships. I put my hard-earned energy once again in someone who did not deserve me. It took me a very long time to realize no matter how available I am and how much I love, I can only fix myself and *no* one else!

Ben needed a really good therapist, not a good girlfriend. He used to tell me he spent quite a bit of time in the foot doctor's and back doctor's offices. He would have really benefited from a head doctor. Staying and trying to fix the wrong man will only prevent us from meeting the right one.

I lead a very busy life. My daughters and I get together as much as possible, meeting for lunch or dinner, concerts, getting manis and pedis and doing yoga. I'll never forget the introductory, two-hour Pilates/pole dancing class we took in Manhattan. It was a lot of fun, even though I was the oldest in the class and got quite dizzy after my first spin around the pole. To be honest, trying to pole dance was on my bucket list.

Speaking of bucket lists, I also wanted to stomp grapes like they did in Italy. A winery upstate had a Lucille Ball look-alike contest. They had this large vat of purple grapes to stomp on. After removing my toe ring and sanitizing my feet, I stepped in the vat. It was a little weird and ticklish at first, but after a few notes of the Sicilian song "Che La Luna" with everyone dancing and switching in each other's arms, I had a blast.

One of my favorite memories is when my daughters and I went to Florida for a few days after Christmas. It was my Christmas present from them. It was so wonderful to actually have our schedules synch at the same time for a few days away. The last time I traveled with them, I was handing them coloring books and crayons and drinks in little boxes. I saw the first hotel they chose on-line and thought it was great, until they told me the bathroom was surrounded by glass, shower and throne, everything for all to see. Now, my daughters and I are very close, but sometimes you need a little privacy. They changed hotels before we got there and the second hotel choice was amazing. We were upgraded to an oceanfront room when they heard we were celebrating my oldest daughter's thirtieth birthday. We had left New York just in time. It was below zero in New York and when we arrived in Miami it was seventy-eight degrees. It was pure sun and fun. We ran on the beach in the morning and had reflexology while relaxing on our beach chairs having coconut water from fresh coconuts. We went to fabulous restaurants on recommendations from their friends and went to a club where we saw the same club drama with young girls crying in the bathroom for some reason or another—probably about a breakup.

While on the beach one day at the swanky hotel, a security guard came over to us.

The gentleman told me to watch my Louis Vuitton bag.

He said his wife has the same one and that it was a popular bag that got stolen a lot. I thanked him and we laughed when he left. Apparently, I had a really good knockoff. I will always treasure the memory of that trip with my daughters.

My friends have all been wonderful throughout the years (You all know who you are!) I am very fortunate to spend weekends in the summer at my friend's house in Cape May, hanging out at the beautiful beach and then dinner and dancing at night. I also spend weekends at my friend's house in Connecticut—hiking, canoeing, dinner, and drinks, whatever—grateful to be together. I also spent many vacations with friends in Vero Beach and Fort Lauderdale. We go on a girlfriend trip twice a year that is a lot of fun. Bingo games upon bingo games and gambling for a long weekend. We play for $10,000 games, which is very nerve-racking. One Saturday I was actually waiting for one number 069. My girlfriend saw it on the monitor and we couldn't yell bingo until they called the number. Well, I couldn't yell anything because the blood drained from my face and she said I was as white as a sheet. I was speechless, which very rarely happened to me. I remember saying *God, don't let me have a heart attack, so I can actually enjoy winning this.* My girlfriend yelled for me so loud we did not hear someone else yell. We were very appreciative to split the $10,000 with someone else. At our hotel room I threw the money all over the bed. Years later, I actually won the $10,000 alone. This time I was able to scream bloody murder all on my own.

We are all partners and share whatever we win. My friends are all a reminder that loving relationships are much broader than just one person. They have included me in everything they do. I don't know where I would be without them today. I tell them all the time how very lucky they are to have found someone that they are happily spending many years together with.

I do enjoy my alone time to work out, read and take my dog on long walks, but at times, I felt like something was missing. One December day comes to mind. I was in a cosmetics/perfume store buying some gift cards. I overheard (who am I kidding—I was listening) this guy telling his friend that he bought his girlfriend some fine perfume and how she deserves much more for putting up with him. I then had a meltdown in aisle five. I found myself on a very long line paying for an $88 perfume that I certainly did not need. Merry Christmas to me!

The Christmas season is a little rough with all the songs about mistletoe and Mommy kissing Santa. Of course, after Christmas comes New Years Eve. Wouldn't it be great to have someone to go out with on New Year's Eve?

Here's a story of another website disaster. I must have seemed like a wonderful catch to Marco. By the second date he was "honey this and honey that" to me and wanted to get off of the dating website to see where it was going. (Keep that in mind.) Marco was Sicilian and Irish, cute and with a nice build. He bragged about his numerous tattoos, his goatee and pinky ring but, apparently, he was as not as forthcoming as he seemed.

At first, I was very enthusiastic about him. He called when he said he would call, seeming to enjoy a lot of time with his family and friends. He seemed to want to do a lot of things with a partner that he had missed out on for the last few years. I told my family and friends about him, as I had a good feeling. However, my good feeling didn't last long!

Let me list some of the bullshit he said to me;

- "I am not into myself. I am enthusiastic (that was a new one, and I thought I heard them all.);

- "I need to find someone who appreciates me;"

- "My mom keeps asking me if I spoke to you and when we are meeting;"

- "I give flowers to girls for no reason" (this is a RED FLAG; there is something wrong if you have to sell yourself);

- "I like all kinds of music, food and sports;"

- "I can come to the Bronx, I am the man and old school;"

- "I will pick you up at the train station sometimes after work or I will meet you in the city, go to dinner and you will not have to come home on the train or bus;"

- "Let's be Facebook friends;"

- "Wow, we only live twelve minutes apart;"

- "I met a girl once who would not date me because I was Sicilian. Can you imagine?;" "You look just like your photo on the website, and others don't (nice compliment, but, overboard with the charm);

- "I was checking out your ass when you got up. I am an ass man." (He sure had the ASS part right);

- "I am affectionate, attentive and respectful;"

- "I don't want to just hook up;"

- "I work out about two hours a day—arms this day, legs this day" (ready to puke yet?);

- "At the end of the month we are having a family dinner. I know my mom will want you there;" and

- "My picture on the website had my abs more cut than now; that was last summer" (no lie).

Every morning he sent a good morning text followed by texts in the afternoon and long phone conversations at night. After the first dinner date, he made plans for another dinner date and he was hell-bent on going out for New Year's Eve. He could not wait to go out New Year's—dancing, take pictures, whatever.

The night before New Year's Eve, Marco told me he would be wearing boots and jeans. He said he may have to stay over since there might be drunks on the road. He didn't drink (he had issues with alcohol years ago) and lived twelve minutes away. I told him I was sorry, but I wasn't ready for him to stay over. He said sure, no problem. He said he would text me in the morning. We had 7:00 p.m. dinner reservations.

The next morning came and no text. It was no big deal. I figured he was running errands and he had said he was going to take a nap. I sent a text to him at 1:00 p.m. and received no answer. That was odd because usually he sent a text right back or called. There was no word, so by 4:00 I called. It went right to voicemail and all of a sudden I thought, *was this asshole standing me up on New Year's fucking Eve?*

Something told me to check Facebook and Marco had ghosted me. I guess he thought I would post something. We never did get to take pictures. Either he did not like that he could not sleep over or he had a wife or girlfriend that would check the website, Facebook and his cellphone or both. I cancelled dinner reservations, took my makeup off, and was sleeping by 8:00.

If he was any kind of decent human being, he could have sent a text or called that he was sick, something came up, etc. How could you do this to someone on New Year's Eve? Not to be dramatic, but I would have liked to start my new year off on a good note. My friend said the only excuse for him was if his name was in the obituary that day. I agreed with that!

I would have loved to call his mommy and say the reason your poor son can't find a decent girl is because he is a fucking asshole!

A few weeks later he sent me a message through the dating website. Marco had a new photo and new bio. I can't say that surprised me. He stated he was sorry about what happened. A few hours after that when I didn't respond, he said, he guessed I was still mad at him.

BLOCKED for good.

About a year later I went on another website for shits and giggles and there he was with his Mom—shirtless and still showing off his abs and tattoos.

I attend mass every Sunday and one day while in church

the priest said they desperately needed catechists for all the grade levels in their Catholic School. I was only available on Saturday mornings, so I volunteered and "answered my calling." I was all set to make fun crafts and crosses out of popsicle sticks and decorate bags to fill for the poor at Thanksgiving. Little did I know that at the age of fifty-two I'd be back to school for Catechist Formation classes, completing Level I and Level II in two years. I took classes online, in schools and in churches. I had to have a background check and be certified in CPR. I attended Catholic school as a child and the classes I attended reaffirmed my faith. I got just as much out of teaching, as my students got in learning. Teaching religion to first graders for five years also brought much laughter into my life. I tried very hard to make their first year of religious education a great one. Weather permitting, we walked down a little hill on Saturday morning to church, before I started my class. Some of their families did not attend church regularly, so I tried to take them there as much as possible. Regardless, if they did not attend mass, I told them God was always there for you, wherever you are, to pray and speak to. When you have faith you have everything. They took turns lighting a candle each week and prayed for family members, friends, the deceased and, of course, their pets.

I told my classes that when they sing at mass that is also a form of prayer. As they say, children say the funniest things. When I asked the children if they say prayers before they have dinner, little Brian raised his hand and proceeded to the front of the class to recite his prayer. He said his dad taught him the prayer. We all waited patiently and he simply said, "Every night Dad says "Bon Appetit!" Not the prayer I expected but, adorable just the same. When doing a craft one day, one of the Priests came in to sit in on my class. While making sheep with cotton balls, one of the children told Father that we should follow Jesus, like the sheep follow the shepherd. I thought to myself, "Wow this is good! The class is really paying attention" and then Alexa had to add that her mom said "If we don't follow Jesus, we are all going to hell!" I think I turned red, but Father just laughed. Give them some time to talk before class and you really have to brace yourself for what they might say. One child told me that her father would be a little late picking her up because he and her mom were divorced and her dad was going to try to squeeze in the gym and a haircut while she was in religion class. I couldn't believe that they spoke about having boyfriends and girlfriends in their first grade classes. They should only know what lies ahead in the dating world!

So many of my friends used to say, they couldn't believe I never met anyone at church through the years. Well, one day this guy I saw at early masses seemed to know my friends who I sat with and we all started talking. Sean asked them later on if I was with someone and they said no. How nice it would be to go to celebrate mass with someone on Sundays. Hallelujah! After speaking to him for a while, I found out he was very religious, sending the statue of the Virgin Mary to his mom in another state and reciting one of St. Paul's letters to the Corinthians. I was impressed. (It was only later that I learned he loved himself as much as he loved God, if not more.)

He said he didn't have a car and he lived locally, so I drove us to a club one Saturday night. We danced and had a great time. He was a good dancer. Somehow, I could not have seen myself driving Mr. Daisy around everywhere. His brother also lived locally. I wondered why he didn't ask him to borrow his car once to take a date out. He had much to say about himself but, never asking about my children, job or anything.

Sean was trying to get another job, make more money, see his mom, make amends with his siblings… on and on and on. I guess he missed the week the sermon at church was about being self-centered. Amen. On the second date at the diner he had gotten a ride from his brother. This is when he confessed that he lost his license a year ago due to a DWI but, he would be getting it back shortly. Oh, and he had an ex-girlfriend still living in his apartment until she had money to move out. If he took a girl to his place, does the ex-girlfriend stay in her room? Did she sit with them? Was she in her room with a guy? Holy shit! Are you kidding? That was too much for me.

About a year later, I still saw Sean walking around my town (no wheels yet?) and I saw him in church sitting with the ex-girlfriend and food shopping with her on a Saturday. Whenever I saw him at mass or in the store after that, he kissed me hello, said God bless me and he asked to go out again saying that he and the girl were not really together. I guess he figured God will forgive him if he was a habitual liar.

I've spoken to many couples and they always said one thing that kept them together was that they made each other laugh. I have always had a great love for making people laugh and smile and I love to tell my stories and stories of others.

To my detriment or not, I have always been an "open book," wear-my-heart-on-my-sleeve type of person. I remember even considering going into the stand-up comedy field but realized, I would rather write about my experiences. I consider myself to be quick-witted and often times I crack myself up. I believe it is good to be able to laugh at yourself.

They say children laugh 300 to 400 times a day, but grown-ups only laugh about fifteen. However, I also know adults that laugh a great deal when intoxicated. They say laughter is great for your immune system and your brain. It helps people relieve tension, stress and form bonding relationships. I have a great appreciation for the power of healing in laughter. When I was a child my desk was always switched in the class room away from other chatty classmates like myself. I loved to tell jokes and could never shut up. I was given the name "MotorMouth" by my classmates. Some of my favorite funny people are Lucille Ball in *I Love Lucy*, Fran Drescher in *The Nanny* and of, course, Curious George, as himself.

I did not get in much trouble growing up (I was a good Catholic girl). I however, always found Lucy, the Nanny and George to be very interesting and funny and they were always in trouble. Never did I think that all of my years of dating and friends and acquaintances dating experiences would bring such laughter. What a concept being with someone who can make you laugh when you are down and laughs with you when you are up. Along with the laughter also came the tears. Remember, some dates were not meant to turn into relationships for whatever reason. It feels like rejection when they do not call, but after a few dates, how can they reject you? They really don't even know you. This is certainly not a sign that there is something wrong with us. Don't we pass on certain people that we feel are not right for us? Sometimes, though, it still stings. In retrospect, I thank God for stepping in and putting an end to some of my poor choices. He always knows what is better for me than I know myself. On a good note, frequent experiences with the wrong man or woman teach you what you want and don't want the next time around. Shouldn't dating later in life bring fun, romance, excitement and laughter and take the crisis out of "midlife"?

One date I had was quite humorous.

Dennis' wife Casey decided she did not want him anymore, but he did not know she did not want anyone else to have him either. When he planned a date (she found out after interrogating their nine-year-old daughter) she would come up with some excuses as to why he had to watch their daughter that night. Dennis took care of his daughter, every other weekend and one night during the week. She was a wonderful manipulator. It is no wonder children grow up with so many issues with a parent like that.

She was always in need of more money. Nothing was ever enough. It didn't help either when from time to time she threatened that he would not be able to see his daughter. Dennis was a great dad and sometimes included me on their weekends together. My weekends were usually jammed with errands, grocery shopping, and nail or hair appointments. As sweet as it would be playing board games and making cupcakes, that was not the life for me. My girls were grown. Been there, done that.

One weekend we planned to go away and for some reason Casey could not take care of their daughter. The weekend was a no-go. I certainly understand that children come first, but this could be the drama he deals with until his daughter is older and makes her own decisions.

I felt sorry for him, but I think because he was afraid to speak up to his ex-wife, matters just kept getting worse. I hear of many people that are afraid to speak up for fear of getting brought back to court, getting custody taken away, not seeing their children, having them be mistreated or other reasons. In my opinion, no matter what the other partner says, they are still the child's mother or father. I would not want to go through life hating either parent because the other bad-mouthed them! We mutually decided this relationship was not going to work.

An attorney I worked for was kind enough to send me to Rockland Community College for a two-year paralegal program that he paid for. I regretted not going to college when I was young so, of course, I enrolled. I was forty-seven at the time and thought I would be the oldest in the class. A gentleman behind me told me he was a doctor and, at sixty-two years old, he decided to go into law. Talk about a great love and ambition for education!

One day I parked my car a few blocks away from the law firm to do some studying on my lunch hour. I had three finals coming up and was under pressure. While eating my sandwich, I heard sirens and, in a flash there were two cop cars surrounding my car. Holy shit! I got so scared. The officer asked if he could smell what I was drinking, Ah, frigging water? He asked what I was doing there and I told him. I told him he could call the lawyer I worked for if he didn't believe me. He knew the attorney I worked for. Apparently, someone in the house I was sitting in front of called the police because they saw a suspicious person was parked outside of their house. Drama always follows me!

I have done a lot of traveling in my life. When I was married we visited Hawaii, California, Cancun, Las Vegas, Bermuda, Seattle and Montana. Later on I traveled to Aruba, Las Vegas again and some beautiful islands in the southern Caribbean. On the top of my bucket list was visiting Italy. I was so fortunate to go to Italy, France and Spain with my cousins at the age of fifty-six. It would have been great to go to Italy with a lover, since it's such a romantic place, but, I didn't want to take the chance in waiting for that to happen while my life passed me by. The trip was everything I hoped it would be and more. It had the best of history, food, and scenery. You name the gelato flavor, I ate it! We ate almonds and olives from the trees in Palma de Mallorca, Spain. They were like no other I have ever tasted. I would have loved to spend more time in Tuscany and lived like Frances from the movie *Under the Tuscan Sun*, but there was so much to see.

Before the trip, I worked with tapes, books and a tutor to teach me to speak Italian (which was another item on my bucket list). She was a great tutor who taught at the local high school for many years. Although many speak English in Italy, I was happy learning the basics. I mastered the most important three words of all time Dove' el bano, where is the bathroom?

It is so funny how life is. Five years before the Italy trip one of my cousins and I went to Las Vegas. I won a little on my *Wizard of Oz* slots, so the next day at the Venetian Hotel we took the gondola ride (my treat). I told her that is was probably the closest I would ever get to Italy. Who knew that five years later she and I would really be going to Italy. Now at sixty-two, I am writing my first book. Better late, than never.

I heard that people meet at all sorts of places—funeral homes, supermarkets and at the gym. I have been to many funerals and did not have any interest in anyone, except the poor person that passed away and his or her family. As for the supermarket, I want to shop and get in and out. I have been a member of gyms for many years and believe me, I am not attractive looking after an hour of spin class. Then again, if they asked me out at the gym, with me being all sweaty and my hair in a ponytail, they will think I'm the cat's pajamas on a date after getting all dolled up.

Like many women I know, I was more focused on being liked than doing the liking. A friend said I was in love with being in love. This was something for me to think about. Even though there was no connection many times, I had a nice enough time. You never knew when one person sitting across from you could become a friend and introduce you to someone fantastic in the future.

I have heard so many stories of dating throughout the years. In college I met a girl who I really admired. We spoke about blind dates and she told me her story. She thought she spotted her date waiting on the sidewalk before she parked the car.

She yelled out "Hi, are you so and so?." He said yes. He looked nothing like he specified in his bio. A photo from a month prior to the date showed him as being tall, thin and with a full head of hair. His description of himself could not have been any further from the truth. I love when you get photographs of what people looked like ten or twenty years ago! Hell, we all looked good back then.

Sometimes, fortunately people do look better in person. How could you explain a large weight gain, going bald and shrinking in a month before you meet? Needless to say, she sped off and never looked back.

This one was not a high school reunion. This was much more fun and intriguing. I wondered what he would say about how I looked after twenty-five years and what he would look like now. Luckily, we both thought each other looked the same—with a few wrinkles here and there.

I met him at the beach when I was seventeen years old. I remember wearing a white bikini. That was probably the last year I ever wore a bikini. No, not really, but I just had a depressing moment thinking about it. He was a very handsome lifeguard and we dated for about two years. He was my first real love. We had two great summers together. We were always at the beach in the day, attending parties at night and going to many concerts. He was also a drummer in a band, so I was his groupie. He was always the perfect gentleman. When we walked on the sidewalk, he would always walk on the street side. He said it was in case a car veered off the road a little then he would be the one to get hit.

About twenty-five years later, he ran into my parents in their neighborhood and asked if they still lived at my old house. He told them he had married and got divorced and he did not have any children. My parents told him I had two daughters and I was also divorced. They were on their way to my house for a block party and he gave them his number for me to call.

After finding the number in the garbage in the tray of eaten lasagna (it was a crazy day), I called him and referred to myself as the blast from the past. We talked for about two hours and agreed to meet that week at a mall for dinner.

While driving to meet him, I wondered to myself if this was fate. We were both single. Was it meant for us to be together after so long? How many people meet with their first love after twenty-five years?

It was a Tuesday night in September, when we spotted each other in front of the mall. We couldn't stop talking and looking at each other as we walked in to have dinner. The waitress kept coming back and forth trying to get our food order, but we had so much to catch up on, who could order? We also shared many photos from over the years. He said he remembered me breaking up with him, but we didn't remember why.

He told me that a few weeks after we broke up, he had mailed me a pair of sexy platform shoes to make amends. (I love shoes!). I never received them, or my mom confiscated them and never told me he sent them. My parents really liked him but were afraid I was too young to get serious with someone. He was twenty-three when I met him. He had many options to pursue and quit his lifeguard job and went on to work at his dream job.

The crazy part is, after all those years the chemistry was still there. We saw each other here and there for the next year. He lived an hour away and worked different shifts. We went to dinner, dancing and attended concerts, like when we were young. We both had a great love of music.

When he came to my house and met my older daughter, he was shocked. He said Erica, then seventeen, looked just like me when we dated when I was seventeen. It was surreal.

He retired, moved out of state and he had asked me to come to live with him, but I was not ready to leave my children and my family. Whenever I visit friends where he lives or he visits New York, we try to get together.

There is no love as special as first love, no pain as painful, no feeling as elegant, no comfort as beautiful, no separation as truthful, and no tears as scary.

Back to the drawing board, as they say.

Before I begin this story, let me share that I worked numerous years for a weight loss organization and have a great deal of compassion for people's struggle with losing weight. When people say, "Oh I just lost a pound. It was probably water," I would say, "Water, blood, fat, whatever—a loss is a loss and a pound is a pound. Better it is in the down direction, then up." I would take a weight loss any way I could get it. When I had my hysterectomy, I asked the doctor how much my uterus, cervix, and ovaries weighed. After he gave me a look like I was nuts, he told me they weighed seven pounds.

I started working at this organization with my own struggles many years prior.

After a while those "slenderizing black clothes" just didn't cut it anymore. Who could forget those all-you-can-eat buffets that I attended and ate like it was my last meal. I remember my dad weighing himself every day when I was a child, so I thought this was normal. I would weigh myself on my home scale in my bathroom, moving it from the tile to the carpet to get a reading of weight I was happy with. I was getting so neurotic I would have dragged it to the damn driveway if I liked what the number displayed. Although I ran the first seven months of my pregnancy, I gained forty pounds with each of my children. I remember the girls at work asking what I had for lunch. I told them it was a piece of chicken and some fruit chunks. They said it looked like "a side of beef." Okay they were big pieces. I, of course used the "I'm eating for two excuse."

Today I work very hard trying to eat right and exercise every day—running, spinning, weight lifting and doing yoga. Even though I do all this, a few years ago a doctor told me during a bone density test I had the beginning signs of osteopena. I was told to take a certain medication that would help or perhaps reverse the bone loss. I also ate more dairy for the calcium. However, when I went to have the prescription filled, I was told it costs $165. For that price, my bones should be as strong as a ten year old. I thought maybe it was for a year.

Nope. The dosage was one pill a month. It was for one itty bitty pill. Fortunately, I had a friend who worked for a doctor who was throwing them away because the company sent too many to them. I used them for two years and lo and behold, the bones improved. I still exercise and lift weights though.

On this particular date, I did not know what to do when my date could hardly fit in the booth at the diner. I tried to move the table. He wiggled in, but I had anxiety over how the hell to get him out of there later. I guess he has been in this situation before. When we were leaving he wiggled around and glided himself out. This gentleman said in his bio that he had a few extra pounds on him. If people lie in their bio about weight, hair, height, whatever, what kind of a relationship will flourish if you start off with a lie? I think some things can be overlooked while others cannot. Is being honest too much to ask?

We spoke in the parking lot before saying goodbye. He told me there were no bells or whistles going off on that date. I wanted to say we should have gone to a frigging carnival if he had wanted to hear bells and whistles. I was dumbfounded. I thought, *how rude; just say goodbye and never call me again.* I had plenty of dates where there were no bells or whistles sounding but, I was kind and considerate in how I handled it. I believe sometimes you have to give someone a chance or two and not expect a grand parade right from the start.

Lastly, he said, "You know, Annette, you remind me of my aunt Esther." I said thank you. I did not ask him why I reminded him of his aunt because I was still trying to process the insult of the no bells or whistles. I will never know if looking like Aunt Esther was a compliment or an insult. On the drive home, I wondered if his aunt was young, old, pretty, homely, frumpy or sexy. I chose to believe Aunt Esther was some really hot mama which was better for my self-esteem!

5.

Second Marriage ... Almost

I *met a great guy named Angelo after my divorce. He lied* about his age for the first few weeks, thinking I wouldn't go out with him because he was fourteen years older than me. He had two children and two granddaughters at the time. He was very energetic, caring and liked to go out a lot. We went dancing, to dinners, movies, bowling, you name it. We also attended a lot of business dinners with people he worked with. We would take long car rides on the weekends, having snacks in the car while listening to Italian music. He loved to shop which was a rare find in men that I have dated. He and I traveled and cruised to Aruba, Florida, Puerto Rico and the southern Caribbean. We got along very well and so did our families and friends. He had a heart of gold. On numerous Valentine's days he would have roses delivered to my office and chocolate covered strawberries for all of the girls. I believed he was my soul mate.

I was getting a second chance on love and marriage. I

hoped this one would last a lifetime! He proposed to me after six months of dating, and, of course, I said yes. My mom thought this relationship was moving pretty fast, but were older now, so why wait? We planned to marry in May, two days after my birthday. My friends held a beautiful bridal shower for me. Along with all of the wedding plans we decided to take a cruise to the Caribbean. He asked me if we should take insurance out on the trip. I said, "Oh no, what could happen? "No need to!" Those were the famous last words.

Then my world came crashing down when he suffered a heart attack the day before the wedding. The ambulance called me as I was getting my daughter who was eight at the time ready for school. I rushed her to my friend's house. While speeding to the hospital, I thought, *was this some kind of sick joke?* Busting into the emergency room doors, I was so scared. *Would he die? Did he have anxiety because of the wedding, a blockage, what?* I was met by the nurse asking for his identification. I was out of my mind and told her, "He is who he says he is!"

When I called my mom from the hospital and told her Angelo had a heart attack, she said, "Angelo who?" I guess she could not fathom something like this ever happening, let alone the day before our wedding.

When the doctor was telling me about his medical condition, all I could think about is how am I going to cancel a wedding tomorrow with 150 people. My head was saying "IS THIS DOCTOR FUCKING KIDDING ME? I HAVE TO GET MARRIED TOMORROW. PEOPLE WERE FLYING IN

FROM CALIFORNIA. I PAID $800 TO GET ANNULLED
SO I COULD GET MARRIED IN THE CATHOLIC
CHURCH AGAIN! HOW DO I CALL THE BAND, THE
GUESTS, THE FLORIST?" I actually asked the doctor if he
could sedate Angelo and he could sit in a wheelchair and
we could get married and then I would take him back to
the hospital. Like I said, I was out of my fucking mind. The
doctor said he had three main arteries clogged and needed
bypass surgery. He made it through, which is more than I can
say for the wedding.

When crying to my mother she said "These things
happen." I said who do you know that this happened to? What
is a mother to say? I know she was just trying to soften the
blow. His first wedding was very small, so this wedding had
150 guests on the list. I drove to the catering hall with a friend
and my future husband's sister to get the place cards, wanting
to not forget to call anyone that was invited. The flowers and
food were to be prepared the next day and the catering hall,
being very understanding, gave back the deposit, in the hopes
we would just reschedule when he was well again. Instead of
preparing for my wedding day, I was calling all the guests to
tell them the news and, of course, after saying he had a heart
attack, I rushed to say he was alive—although I wanted to
fucking kill him.

The next day flowers and gifts arrived from people who
could not be at the wedding and from people who heard the
bad news and wanted to say they were sorry. My living room
looked like a funeral home. I finally got the band on the
phone late that night. People were saying, "Oh you're the girl

whose fiance' had a heart attack the day before the wedding?"
I was the talk of the town.

On the night that was supposed to be my honeymoon
Angelo told me to go home and rest as his bypass surgery
was scheduled the next day. My girlfriends and I went to
the nearest bar and got shit-faced. What else is a girl to do?
Calling on one's support system is essential for survival.

Since we never did take that cruise insurance out, we had
to fight with the cruise line to get our money back. Although,
we sent all the hospital documents and proof of the surgery,
they reimbursed us only half of the cruise amount to be used
in six months. We did take the cruise—along with Hurricane
George. We were the last flight out of New York and flew
to Puerto Rico to sail the Caribbean. It was beautiful until
George came. The winds were horrendous, the water came out
of the pools, the cabana boys were gathering the lounge chairs
to take in so nobody would get hit with them. We then all
had to remain inside. I was hoping Angelo didn't have another
heart attack with all this drama. We caught a few nice days
and then something happened to one of the guests. We were
too far from shore so a helicopter came and sent down a basket
for them to put the man in and haul him into the helicopter.
The basket came down and was swaying from side to side.
They got him in and then his wife held onto a rope and they
pulled her up. Petrified to get in the little basket, I would have
just dropped fucking dead on the ship. They announced later
that the gentleman was in Miami Hospital and would be fine.

Between the heart attack and this cruise, I thought I had
some kind of curse over my head.

After returning home from all the drama, we postponed the wedding for six months. It should have been enough time for him to get back on his feet and be healthy, but he changed his mind about marrying. He was concerned about getting sick again in the future and me having to take care of him. I said what if that happened to me, would he have taken care of me? Wow, how God's intervention came just in the nick of time.

I remember spending my lunch hours in the car listening to our favorite songs and crying myself to sleep in my bedroom, trying to escape the pain I was feeling. I spent countless nights not sleeping, wondering what went wrong, could it have been worked out? My mom's advice was for me "to snap out of it." I wish it was that easy. That was one engagement ring that went back and forth more times than I care to remember. It was a beautiful round, raised diamond. Many people told me I should have kept the ring and sold it. It was not the ring I ever wanted, but the love and a beautiful relationship was more important to me. All I can say is that ship has passed. We are still friends and when we think about all the drama, all we can do is find humor in the situation and shake our heads and laugh.

When they say some things were not meant to me, believe it.

6.

The One That Left the Biggest Hold in My Heart

This was probably the hardest part I had to write. It brings
up bad, painful memories, but I am compelled to share
this. It happened a long time ago and took me the longest of
times to get over. I felt like I didn't recover from a love lost
or a failure of a relationship, but from warfare. It is amazing
that the heart makes no noise when it cracks!

This man was the only man I can say loved me uncondi-
tionally—*or so I thought*. I was a lot older, having wrinkles and
other things that he wouldn't have until he got older. Phillip
made me feel like the most beautiful and sexiest girl in the
world. It took a long time for me to realize that was probably
the reason I kept going back to him over the years. At that
time, I could seriously have called myself the Holler Back
Girl. He would turn on the charm and throw a few crumbs

my way. It was like he had some kind of hold on me. I made one excuse after the other about his erratic behavior. As a dear friend put it, the biggest hole was left because at the time he was filling a big void in my life.

While at a bar one night with friends, I went out to have a cigarette and started talking to Phillip, who was also out for a smoke. He was very flirtatious and I had this tingle inside—attraction, whatever you want to call it. He asked for my number but did not call until two weeks later. We spoke for hours. One night he mentioned how "you have to connive to survive." I had selective hearing and was not listening.

We spoke every few days and became friends. Some days he would call so many times, at all hours. I thought he was really into me but he never seemed to have any boundaries. Some nights we would talk on the phone for hours, not two or three but, five or six. I could not remember what the hell we spoke about for all that time.

I used to love to watch him fall asleep, until I fell out. We used to slightly tickle each other under our arms and see who could go longer without laughing. It was so silly, but I was so happy.

He was away for the summer at a friend's house, fishing and swimming, so we got together when the summer was over. He was, by far, the youngest man I ever dated. It was like the movie when Stella got her groove back. The chemistry was crazy. (Or I was just crazy). We could not sit near each other without having some part of our bodies touching. When we slept together our bodies were always entwined like a pretzel.

I really missed that for a long time. I would circle his lips with my finger over and over. I would kiss him anywhere. I didn't care where the hell we were.

He was an expert at seduction, but he was also an expert manipulator, distorting facts to suit his own agenda. Did you ever look in someone's eyes and see right through them? I wish I possessed that power. I would have saved myself from much heartache. Phillip never saw in himself what I saw—his big heart and his potential. However, he would never come to realize any of this because he was a narcissist. This is something I knew nothing about. I had never met a person like this before. Unfortunately, I didn't realize it until it was all over. The pieces of the puzzle came together and things started making sense after so many years passed. His father had never been in his life. His mother was out doing her own thing, and he had a lot of anger issues as a child. I overheard two girls at the gym asking each other why he was always so angry. I wasn't paying attention to any of this. Because of his emptiness and self-hatred, he felt he was entitled to drain the life out of everyone around him. I believe as long as people keep blaming their mothers, fathers, sisters, brothers, ex-girlfriends, whoever, they will never be free and heal emotionally.

His friend always joked to him that whenever he called me or however many times he called or drunk-dialed me, I would always answer the phone. That is what he loved about me; that I was always there for him. However, he was only emotionally available to me when he needed or wanted something. I worried about his problems and his well being. He asked me if I could help him get a job? I guess I had a lot of time on my hands to spend on him. I was on the back burner. I felt with all my love I could make him better. Was he caring, controlling or being needy and selfish? At the beginning narcissistic never entered my mind. I did feel he cared, but sometimes the way someone cares may not be the care and love that you need. He could have had a younger, prettier or sexier girl, but he wanted me. I could not help thinking at the beginning, *Is he too young for me? Am I too old for him? What would people think?* I told him many times to get over himself because he acted so full of himself with high self-esteem, but nothing could be farther from the truth. I just didn't get it at the time. Hell, it felt great so I just went with it. Phillip never wanted children and at that point my shop was closed. I didn't need him to marry or support me.

When I was with him I felt so much younger and carefree. The hours of making out were bliss. I felt so safe in his arms. I remember thinking, *Oh Lord will this guy ever go to sleep? Hell no!!! What was I thinking? Lucky me!* Even though there was a big age difference—he was nineteen years younger than me—we seemed to have a lot in common. We loved the same foods, music, classes at the gym and cooking together. We would cook, have a lot of wine and dance around the kitchen for hours. I think when you truly love someone you would walk miles just to be together, even if it's for a little while.

Sheryl Crow has a song called "My Favorite Mistake." It was certainly not my favorite, or biggest one but—yes, I understand!

Since he was changing jobs, not sure what he wanted to be when he grew up, he did not have extra money to take me to dinner. I would rather stay home and order in. It was like no one else existed in the world when we were together. He also said he loved my dog. He insisted on walking her without a leash sometimes. I would go nuts. It was another part of the control he needed. When he stayed over I would get a little crazy because he would throw his keys on the floor, his shoes in the kitchen, and his jacket on the couch. Everything in my house has its place. I guess when he lived at home, he was used to his sister and mother picking up after him.

$\sim$

One time Phillip invited me to go camping on a Sunday night. I had to work the next day, but who cared. I was trying to be spontaneous like younger people are. What do I know about camping, coming from the Bronx? I thought there would be a port-a-potty, however, the nearest tree was my bathroom. UGH. I had the wine and toilet paper. He pitched the tent and made sandwiches. He made a fire and the weather was perfect. I started to feel my arm getting very hot and realized the sleeve of my furry coat was on fire. It was certainly not the right coat for camping either, but it was November. Instead of taking the coat off (not thinking, just panicking) we were hitting the sleeve with a blanket. Finally, we put the fire out and the whole side of my coat was charred and smelled of smoke. We were on the top of a mountain and he must have screamed a hundred times how much he loved me and now his life has direction.

He loved how much I loved him. He told me he thought

of marrying me one day. I realized later on that was just another piece of bait for me to go for and hang on to.

We had to get out of the tent due to a very heavy rain and went to sleep in the car a little while. He said not to worry about getting up because he automatically wakes everyday at 5:30. Well, we woke up at 7:00 and I rushed to get home to shower and go to work. I looked like a hot mess by the time I got to Rockland County. It could have been worse as we left all the food out, which professional campers say never to do, unless you want to invite bears. Nevertheless, I had the camping experience.

No matter what I did, I could never understand why he never felt loved enough, appreciated and respected. I never questioned why he was not always available for me.

He loved that I got crazy and frustrated because I could never get what I wanted and needed from him. Things started to unravel very quickly and I needed to run away.

After spending the night in a hotel with him, he proceeded to tell me he was engaged, living with his fiancee' and they were getting married in three months. I felt like I got shot—not once, but twice. While trying to comprehend what he just said and what my next move was, he was saying something about leaving in the middle of the night and not telling me and I should consider myself lucky that he told me the truth.

Oh my God, I remember screaming, *how could you do this to me? I loved you. I gave you everything. I was the only one that ever believed in you..* I called him every name in the book and every other word was FUCK. I didn't know if I should stay and beat the shit out of him. I just keep yelling at him, putting my finger in his face. I told him to never contact me again and asked how could he be so cruel. His face was frozen like a statue. He never uttered a word. It felt like my face was on fire. I was filled with rage that I never felt in my life. When I could not scream anymore I ran out and slammed the door so hard I thought it would come off its hinges. I think I heard him say he was sorry. I ran down the two flights of steps, two at a time, like a murderer was chasing me. Two hours later after driving around trying to figure out what just happened to me, I called my girlfriend and then my therapist, crying hysterically. I couldn't process what was going on. I probably could have used an exorcism to get rid of the rage I felt.

My therapist sorted things out for me after many, many sessions and explained what narcissistic people are capable of doing. I have an uncanny way of rationalizing and analyzing everything. He said sometimes when they have anger management issues stemming from grade school, they also have sociopathic and anti-social disorders. This shit was way over my head. He told me to stay away, change my number, block his number, whatever it took. He suggested I keep very busy. I would write a letter, putting all of my feelings on paper and then rip it to shreds. I also read a lot of self-help books, books about narcissists, and realized my story was not as bad as many others. They easily charm you and suck you back in for as long as they could. I told my therapist that he never would have to worry about us getting back together.

About two years later on a Sunday morning I was at

the gym on the treadmill (the wound all healed, I thought). Phillip walked in and looked at me. I thought I saw a ghost or a monster. I looked the other way and could feel the blood drain from my face. I finished my workout and ran the hell out. I fought with myself whether or not I should change gyms and move to another. I should have moved to another state, let alone, another gym.

A few weeks later on a Sunday night this guy from an online dating site was going to call me. We were texting for a few weeks and were finally going to speak. When I saw the number was unfamiliar, I figured it was him and I picked up. Unfortunately, it was Phillip. I still ask myself why I didn't hang up. I guess I was very vulnerable at the time. I also wanted answers and closure that I never got. From now on, I learned to make my own closure when a relationship dies. He told me the marriage didn't work out (no surprise there) and that she was needy and never trusted him and he divorced her after a year and a half. He could not take her shit anymore. I didn't work for lawyers for nothing, so I did a little searching through the court system online (it's public knowledge) and she (the plaintiff) served him (the defendant) with divorce papers. She got away, lucky girl. I would have loved to hear her side of the story. He wanted to be friends. I was never a big fan of animosity and hiding from people I don't like, so I said whatever. At least I could stay at my gym and hold my head up high.

As I mentioned, I attend church weekly and try to see the good in everyone, if they have any. With this situation, I was trying to do the right thing and not be mean and revengeful. I told myself I have more experience in the relationship department and had relationships a lot longer than he had. I could handle this. I thought I was mentally and emotionally stable to just be friends. Wrong, wrong and wrong again!

We would talk a little here and there. The chemistry was still there and when I watched him help other women at the gym I would be so jealous, sad and insecure. A narcissist loves to watch you rattle. I had read that promiscuity runs wild in narcissistic men. We started back up again. I was still single and time had healed the wounds. I thought, *just maybe, things will be different*. I played the song "Love Will Lead you Back" hundreds of times. He did come back again and again, but, not because of love. He had other motives. They say sometimes giving someone a second chance is like giving them an extra bullet for their gun because they missed you the first time. This was so true. Just when I thought he could not ever hurt me again or hurt me so bad, he did.

After his second or third DWI he went to rehab. I sent him toiletries and snacks, wrote to him and attended the church that ran the rehab program. When he got out he decided to call two days later. I was pissed. I went to the gym and sat on my spin bike while he was across the room talking and laughing with some girl. I had two choices: run like a little baby, giving him satisfaction that he got to me or stay there and endure the pain. I endured the pain, which I hate to say, I deserved. I called and told him to get his families furniture and shit out of my house. He came a few weeks later—with his mother, no less—to take everything out. He always did things when it was convenient for him.

I no longer went to the gym and worked out at home.

I often asked myself what is so intriguing about dating the bad boys, the ones with great looks, bodies, or both. I wonder how many girls wreck their lives up trying to tame these guys.

I only saw what I wanted to see with him. He did do some nice things for me on occasion. In my search for the one person who would change my life, I should have just looked in the mirror. Chalk this up to one of those times when my fantasy wishful thinking replaced reality thinking. I acted on sheer impulse and on the intense physical, emotional and sexual attraction, clouding my good judgment. I admitted the lack of good judgment, not feeling guilty about it and moved on.

Even if you have a lot in common, there has to be some maturity. I thought for a long time he was commitment-phobic, but that was not the case. He always seemed to blame many others for his life. I thought it was just a matter of him needing to grow up. It took me a long time to get it, but I finally did. Sometimes people have to learn things the hard way. This was one of those times for me.

Slowly, but surely, that hole in my heart eventually closed. Note to myself "Never make someone a priority when all you are to them is an option!" Years later I heard he was living with a girl from his past. He would go from girl to girl to take care of his every need, without giving anything in return.

After being in the Bronx for about two years, I received a text saying that he knew he had not been a good friend in the past (I had thought back in the day we were more than that). He said maybe one time we could go to the rehab together and he would like to make a donation. Gee, I wondered why he never went to the rehab on his own to make any such donation? He asked for me to forgive him (as suggested in the AA meetings). I said I forgave him and wished him well. Be good enough to forgive someone, but don't be stupid enough to ever trust them again!

One day I answered my phone without checking the number. I have to remember just because the phone rings, doesn't mean I have to answer it! It was him. He told me he was living alone. I said to myself, thank God she got away from him also. We were the fortunate ones to get away. I have spoken to many women who did not get away fast enough and lost homes, cars and, worst of all children, all in the name of love. I said I had to walk the dog and hung up. I blocked the number, feeling good and healed this time, with or without any closure.

I had to take full responsibility for myself. I grieved the loss of the relationship and made myself strong again.

"I've always liked stories when women save themselves!"

7.

Online Dating

Whether you are eighteen or eighty-eight there's a dating website for you. The first dating site I joined wasn't expensive, but I didn't think it was worth the money. I went onto another site that some friends of mine had said was better and was free. It was funny though, because some of the same faces were also on the first site. I tried about four of them. It was like a part time job. Check messages, check to see if anyone new is on, update your profile at any time or change your picture.

One Saturday I had a lunch date and a dinner date. Feast or famine.

Danny spoke about his job, kids, car, ex-girlfriends, traveling, things he built—you name it. It was like the whole conversation was rehearsed. Every time I opened my mouth to speak, he spoke. I would have liked to talk about my job, family and hobbies. He wasn't interested. This went on for an hour. I could not wait to leave so I could speak to someone.

I couldn't believe he didn't even realize that my mouth never opened, except to eat. It seemed like he had a really good time with himself. If that wasn't bad enough his phone rang every ten minutes. Unless it is your children (they always come first) or, if you are a doctor and have a patient on the operating table, couldn't the call wait? It could have been his friends checking to see how the date was going and if it wasn't going well he could have used the call as an excuse to leave. Regardless, the whole date just cried out, "RUDE!"

Some people wonder why they are always alone. A wonderful, funny girlfriend of mine once said, "That was an hour of my life I can never get back."

A friend of a friend got the okay from me and Herb to exchange our numbers and send a photo. After a long wait and the flu, I met him only to find out he was married and they had been living in different houses that they both owned for the past four years. He spoke about her like they talked often (which I'm sure they probably did) and he had no intention of getting divorced because he was not going to spend the money on attorney's fees.

When I spoke about dating he looked at me like I was from outer space. Apparently, he has not dated in the last four years. I wanted to tell him that I have been dating for quite some time and did not need a meal or companionship that had no potential of going anywhere. Do I have a lot of dating years ahead? Shit, I don't know, but, at least I try.

Before I tell you my friend's story, let me express that I understand that some people do not tell you they are married.

Alternatively, you find out later after you become friends and you are emotionally involved—hook, line and sinker.

Here was a classy guy who was married with an arrangement that they could both see other people. I bet if you called his wife she was not aware of any such dating arrangement Couple's therapists state that less than one percent of the population are really able to have a successful open marriage. I guess he never saw his relationship with his wife as permanent, as he confessed, he had cheated before. To my girlfriend, he was perfect in every way (except for the marriage part). She decided to get involved with him anyway. Besides, he said he was going to leave his wife soon. Herb was the poor, misunderstood husband. He said they are always fighting, there was no intimacy, and they grew apart through the years as they were both very dedicated to their jobs. However, he couldn't leave her because they had to raise their young children and he couldn't tell his parents because they are old. He also didn't want people in the neighborhood to think bad of him, Yadda, yadda, yadda.

We should all take my friend's mother's advice; if the relationship is going nowhere after six months, let it go. But, we don't take that advice and, hence, we look back and wonder what were we thinking and why are were we still in the relationship years later. As the saying goes "You can't work things out, if there is nothing to work with." If and when the day comes that you need a married man to tempt you with romance and then he runs back to his wife, it's the day you may need to enter a self-help class.

Thanks to the technology of Facebook, we found out his kids were out of the house and were in college and his parents have passed away. He and his wife later moved out of that neighborhood and they are still living happily or unhappily ever after. There are so many online descriptions of hopeless romantics. Some have the hopeless part right. A lot of people like to walk on the beach and travel. Speaking of traveling, one gentleman said he didn't like the city, traffic, tolls or crowded places. I guess he never left his town to go to concerts or sports events. One site I was going to go on had so many questions on the application you would have thought you were applying for a job as an astronaut or president of the United States. I got bored and ended my questionnaire, never joining that one.

I understand there is typing involved when you communicate with online dating but, after a while, can we stop typing and speak on the phone? I feel I can get to know someone better after hearing their voice. I deleted far more emails than I answered. I am also not fond of typing all evening. Also, women and men can seem like scholars in a text having a thesaurus and a dictionary nearby.

One guy asked how I was, I said I was doing well. He then asked if I had any tattoos, to which I replied no and he stated he had two. The next question was if I was very sexual. I rolled my eyes (which I am good at) and never replied.

Were there no other questions he could think of asking, like about my family, children or job? While on the subject of tattoos, let me not forget about Peter who took a bus and train to meet me. He did not have a car because he sold it and was planning on moving to Manhattan, where he didn't need one. At least that is the story he told me. He didn't leave himself enough time to travel and was very late but gave me a blow-by-blow of the streets his bus was passing, so I knew he was really on his way. I was getting annoyed since it was a week night and this date didn't seem to be starting until 8:30/9:00. He also had no MetroCard and no change to get on the bus, so he had to stop at the store. It was a hot summer night and he asked me if he could wear shorts for our date. I said sure, wear whatever you want. I thought it was sweet of him to ask me what he should wear. It was 88 degrees and I chose a place where we could eat outside under a canopy.

I soon found out there was nothing sweet about Peter. He wore shorts alright, that looked like he went five rounds with frigging Zorro. His cool, black, cut-off T-shirt showed his huge tarantula tattoo crawling up his arm.

While looking at the menu he asked me what looked good. I said I hadn't had broccoli-rabe in a while. He suggested I should order it because it has a lot of fiber and will "clean me right out." GROSS! Oh my God, who says these things—on a first date no less. He proceeded to dip his bread in the olive oil while it splattered down his shirt. When the check came, I offered to pay my share, like I always do. He said no but, held up the check and loudly said, "It's eighty-nine dollars. How much should I leave for the tip?" I thought I would die. The waiter heard him and I think he wanted to die for me. I told him how much to leave for the tip. Did he just crawl out from under a rock? Does he go out to dinner at all?

At the end of our meal, he asked the waiter for some extra bread and olive oil to take home. What Italian doesn't have olive oil in their kitchen? The kicker was he was going home on the bus and then the train, carrying his olive oil! He tried to kiss me when he walked me to my car and I pulled away. I said I was shy. I guess if I were really into him, I might have thrown him down on the sidewalk. *Next*!

~

While on the subject of eating out, one date, Eddie picked a restaurant on the water. It was a beautiful day and the conversation was going well. The waiter came over and asked if we would like an appetizer and my date said rather loudly, "Oh, we are okay, we are having salads." (I was never not offered an appetizer on a date). He had a Cobb salad and I had four scallops and spinach in my salad, which wasn't very filling. Anyway, I figured, okay maybe a little dessert would suffice. However, when the waiter asked about having dessert my date said again, out loud, "Oh, we're okay. We had the salads." (I was never not offered dessert either on a date). I felt like saying if I had ice cream or a pastry would that have put him over the edge or into bankruptcy? I should have ordered it and said I would pay for it myself. If you cannot afford to eat out, meeting for coffee or a glass of wine would have been fine. When I went home I was starving and had two bowls of cereal.

Some months later I went on a date and we had a glass of wine. It was a place to have tapas and he was looking at the sliders or grilled chicken salad. He told the waiter we would share a salad. *And I was complaining about Eddie just letting me order a salad!* At least I had my own. The other guy told me to take some first (nice gesture), however, there was a handful of lettuce and four pieces of chicken the size of four miniature chocolates. No croutons, cucumbers or tomatoes. In my world, you split something like a sixteen-ounce porterhouse steak and lobster tails. He told me he was worried about girls being gold diggers. Gold diggers? They were certainly not finding gold in his backyard. I wanted to say, judging from our ordering, I would certainly not have expected him to have large amounts of money.

When you think they couldn't get any cheaper, a recent date suggested the diner and it was dinner time, so I figured we'd have dinner. Nope, he didn't offer dinner or a muffin with my coffee. Norman had water. I would have ordered my dinner and paid for it, except I could not prolong the date another minute and ate when I got home.

Of course, my oldest friend Ynette needs to have a story in this book. We had gotten divorced within six months of each other, and we decided to go on a singles cruise around the Statue of Liberty to celebrate our divorces. She always seemed to stumble upon men, just walking in the streets of Manhattan, who start up a conversation with her and then ask for her number. She had worked in Manhattan for a number of years. A few times that I did a bit of walking in the city, was to meet with head hunters and to go on job interviews. I saw some really nice-looking men there. The only thing I stumbled upon was salads for lunch (two croutons, two raisins and a nut) that cost me and arm and a leg.

One night came when she was invited to go out, but just didn't feel like it. On the other side of town, Jonathan's friends were trying to drag him out and he didn't feel like it either. They both gave in to appease their friends and went to the same bar. Both of them were not having a good time and wanted to leave. They stayed with their friends a little longer and then both walked out and walked right into each other. It seemed that they couldn't get out of that place fast enough and walked outside laughing about it. They had a cigarette before they left and talked for about an hour. He asked her to go for Mexican food that week and they have been inseparable ever since. I would meet them to go out and he would buy the both of us roses. One day while in Little Italy in Manhattan we were waiting to get a table and he ran across the street to buy us hats. Mine, of course, was a black and white, pin striped fedora. Not only was Jonathan good to my friend, and her friends, he was wonderful to her beautiful thirty-three-year-old, daughter who has special needs. He is truly the salt of the earth. They have been living together for more than a decade.

~

This dating thing goes both ways. My friend Bobby called me one day and said, "Annette, wait until you hear this story!" He met a woman who said she looked like a talk show host on television. (She was a very pretty woman, I might add). Bobby said that wasn't the reality. He made a reservation at a very nice restaurant. He loves to cook and he has a great appreciation for good food. Bobby got there early and started talking to a couple at another table. He thought nothing of it when his date's niece dropped her off at the restaurant. They had a glass of wine and talked a lot, but she seemed extremely nervous. He asked her if she was alright and she said it was her first date after her husband died three years prior and she had taken two Prozac before she got there to calm her nerves. He thought to himself, *maybe she shouldn't have had the wine.* Too late, because after the wine kicked in she fainted, her head going in her dish of pasta. When the owner revived her with smelling salt, she woke up and puked all over the place. Embarrassed to no end, she gave him her cell to please call her niece. Bobby was sure glad she wasn't getting in his car after that. He couldn't call the niece fast enough to come and take the talk show host home.

In the meantime, he was so embarrassed because the couple at the other table knew it was a first date and were hoping it would go well. I guessed they were just as surprised as Bobby was.

Years later he was introduced to a wonderful woman (who was also widowed) and they hit it off great. Now they are retired and have grown children and grandchildren and love to travel. It means so much when you find someone on the same page as you.

Sometimes it is comforting to hear that men have similar issues like we women do with meeting a nice person. One of my dates was a pleasant surprise. Lou was nice-looking with a great smile. He started a conversation that covered many different topics. When he married his wife, he thought she was not nearly in love with him as she was with the idea of moving out of her house that she shared with her parents. It was another case of following the heart, instead of the head. His wife betrayed him and he was paying child support and maintenance for many years. Even though he had an ugly divorce (how many of them are ever pretty?), he was haunted by happy memories of her. They each spent about $500 in legal fees to fight over a frigging chair that was worth about $10. The spitefulness just went on and on. He did not have a high opinion of woman anymore.

Lou was very lonely and did not feel like going out that much anymore. Just when he believed that he would never find love again and all the romantic stuff is in the movies, Vanessa appeared. He was introduced to her by his friend, who could not stand to see him unhappy any longer. They had a lot in common and were both looking for a mate. Perhaps it was too soon but, they moved in together after a few months. They were so happy doing all these romantic things for each other; rose petals on the bed, sensual music, making coffee for each other in the morning, romantic getaway weekends, red lights in the bedroom, and sexy lingerie. She would even meet him for dinner without wearing underwear, that one he could have left out of the conversation! Then the shit hit the fan, as they say, and he found out she cheated on him with one of his (so-called) friends.

He started to cry when talking about her. I felt so bad for him, but I wanted to say "Forgive me if I'm wrong, but I don't think you are really ready to date yet." Some people just don't want to be alone. I think this relationship was as important to him as oxygen was for his lungs. I think this man lived under the illusion that there was only one perfect person for him. Whether the person is widowed, divorced or was cheated on, some are just not ready to date. An assistant clinical professor at Harvard Medical School believes that for boys to be happy and healthy they must be allowed to have feelings, to show empathy and to be able to express the range of emotions encouraged in girls. It should be no different when they become grown women and men.

~

Whether attached at the umbilical cord, hip or whatever, we can all hope that there are men out there who go out into the world and make it on their own. I have friends whose sons do a lot for their moms. They leave coffee made in the morning, pick up things in the supermarket, among others things and want nothing in return. There are also sons who do nothing for Mommy and want everything in return.

Once I was set up by a friend for a blind date. She thought we would be a good match. He was very funny and she was right. Brandon was a cute guy, younger than me. (You will find throughout this book I dated younger and older then me and I got to the point where I didn't know where the hell to go, nor what age bracket I fell into.) Anyway, he lived with his mother until he could get on his feet (so he said) and he had two young children. I should have been a little suspicious when he told me his brother lived at home too and was in his forties. Brandon made decent money, but I found out he blew all of his money on an expensive car, video games, movies, and trips to Disneyland for him and the kids while mommy maintained the roof over their heads, cooked meals and didn't charge him rent.

We attended a wedding for someone I worked with and it was cute of him to buy two suits and told me to pick the one I liked best. Brandon was a good shoulder to cry on when my grandmother passed away; he was a good listener. He and I went on a cruise to the Bahamas and Disneyland. He was mature in the Bahamas, but Disney was another story. He enjoyed Shrek and Jaws at Universal Studio, but it was a little too much for my liking. He was a great father, but he seemed to get more of a kick out of the movies and games than his children did. Let me add here that I am not much for TV. I'd rather read, speak to friends on the phone or workout. I could not endure another Harry Potter flick. I fell asleep through every one of them. How many are there now? Frankly, I would have rather given birth again—and I've had two C-sections. Unfortunately, not everyone makes a good adjustment from adolescence to adulthood.

Sometimes dating is like a job interview. Let's talk about the photographs people post. One posted a picture of himself from the waist down in his underwear. He couldn't find another picture of himself in his photo albums to make himself look like he had a little class? Another posted himself from the waist down with something bulging out of his jeans. Needless to say we can figure out where their minds were. Guess we know what kind of girl he was looking for. What is with the photos of children? Is it their children? It is them when they were children? All children are beautiful in my eyes, but I would appreciate a more recent photo. I hear the same from men. Women post pictures of themselves ten or twenty years ago. One gal said she was curvy, but he also saw that she was about 100 pounds larger than what she described to him. Some post photos of their dog, cat, motorcycle, or very detailed car and none of themselves. We want to see photos of the person we are going to meet. Now your pet may be adorable, like mine, but I am not going to date Rover or Max.

Save the sunset photos for when we go on vacation. One guy had a photo of himself surrounded by many cats and dogs. Did he work in a kennel? Were they his pets? There are also the ones far away on a boat or skydiving or golfing. A lot of us are more photogenic farther away, but, come on. One guy wore costumes. Was it Halloween every day at his house? Who could tell what the hell he looked like. Last, but not least, when there was no photo where the photo should be, (Is he married?) I, of course, waited until I was divorced before dating, but not many others do the same.

～

When I met Connor he told me he was married—but not. What the hell does that mean?

A mutual friend thought we should meet. Unbeknownst to both of us, we didn't know Connor was still married. If I did know, I wouldn't have met him. Connor explained they both live in the house for financial reasons. His wife—that he is married to, *but not*—ran up $20,000 in credit card debt. When they got married she handed him her bill of $20,000 and said, "You are my husband now; you can pay this." They have their own bedrooms and Connor has a lock on his door because this psycho wife stole money and jewelry from him a few times and ransacked his room. (And I would ever go to that house?) I don't care if they resided in a mansion together and she lived in the east wing and he lived in the west wing, I wanted no part of that living situation. Even if I dated him under the assumption he would be divorced soon (by the way, this is year five and they are still in the courts), he probably would never have money to do anything. He was paying all the house bills and he was responsible for the charge card debt. None of this really matters because his wife would have made me disappear somewhere if she found out he was dating. Did I mention she was also Italian? Bad temper and perhaps cement shoes for me.

My friend, Barb, thought she met the man of her dreams online. They talked every night for hours and seemed to have a lot in common. Every time they make plans to meet, something came up for him. We wondered if he was married (possibly), but he did ask her out on different nights, so maybe he wasn't married. Sometimes the married men forego the Saturday night date because they are with their wives (I just know from experience with another friend). Finally the shoe drops and he tells her he is in a financial bind and asked if she could loan him $5,000? Wow, not even $500. Guess he figured why start low, just go for the full amount. She told him she didn't have that kind of money and so long.

My friend always tells me to "listen to your gut or your red flags." Some women (me) have an uncanny ability to ignore all the warnings being given. Hell, some of those red flags could be flying in my face and I would look the other way. One man comes to my mind as he told me he argued quite a bit with his family and friends. They just didn't understand him, he said. He did admit that not speaking to his daughter-in-law was tough because he had a four-year-old grandson. I wanted to say, *do you think maybe it's you*? Oh well. Let him go through life thinking the whole world is a mess but *not* him.

I do know three couples that are married today, due to the online dating. I attended the beautiful wedding of one of the couples. She has been a great friend of mine for many years. They chatted a little while and then met pretty quickly because it felt so right. They could not be more compatible if they were some scientific experiment.

The bar scene is not that appealing when you are in your fifties and on, but at least you see their faces and what they look like in the present (not some old photo of their glory days) and you talk to them face-to-face. You have to be cautious sometimes of what is hiding behind a computer.

This online dating is really a good thing if you are not able to leave your house. My friend, Fiona, was talking to this guy online for quite some time and he asked her to come over to his house. She was not going to take the chance and go to his house the first time without ever meeting him in person. He was so insistent and she was so adamant about not going there. He finally told her he could not go out because he was under "house arrest." Imagine being under house arrest and still trying to date?

I tried to call guys back when I said I would and just had common courtesy and respect.

I had plans to speak to Stephen on Wednesday night to plan a date on Saturday. However, I was taken to the emergency room by my girlfriend. The local doctor told me he thought my appendix was about to burst. I was getting morphine, and waiting in a little room for a permanent one. Stephen called and I told my girlfriend to answer it. I wanted to tell him what happened before the morphine kicked in. She said she thought I was nuts, but I spoke to him and he said he heard crazy stories to get out of a date before, but this one was the best.

That date never happened as I was in the hospital for a week with pancreatitis. Stephen called my cell every day while I was in there. He also sent flowers to the hospital, only knowing the hospital name, my first name and the floor I was on, which was very sweet. When I was discharged we dated twice but did not seem to have very much in common. He was ready to retire and travel and I had many years of employment ahead of me. I had just started a new job, with no vacation coming for a while.

I also dated many men who were constant complainers. They just date and date and are never happy. I wanted to say, *What would you do if real serious problems occurred in your life?* They complained about their ex-wives being bi-polar and the children having been affected. (That is really sad.) They hate their jobs. Their wives took away their businesses, money, and house in the divorce agreement. Their dogs hate them (seriously). They always have back pain, neck pain, knee pain,

(Any other parts I left out, *those hurt* too). One man actually told me the medication he was on gave him horrible issues with pooping. Holy crap, (pun intended), are you kidding me? That was way too much information, too soon. I can probably venture a good guess that their medicine cabinets are full of medications to keep them happy, make them poop, control blood pressure, and much more. Hail to the younger and healthier men that have condoms, hair gel, toothpaste, pimple cream and even moisturizer in their medicine cabinets.

One younger guy talked about how many women wanted to sleep with him. I wanted to say, *I really don't give a crap*, but I let him talk and have his time in fantasy land.

You start to feel like you are their therapist, the shoulder they need to cry on, and walk away from the date emotionally drained. If I wanted to be a therapist, I would have become one. As they say, I have my own problems to deal with. Save the drama for the fifth date at least.

As hard as dating can be, I could never be with someone because he is adorable, has a great body, has a lot of money, or a prestigious career. Don't get me wrong, none of these are bad things, but I have to care to some degree. What happens to a relationship if Mr. Adorable is not so adorable in ten years or his great body went south or his money runs out or he loses his great job?

People believe that money is power. I spoke to a girl who was all about the man with the money. She met her knight in shining armor, the man of her dreams that would take care of her the rest of her life. Did she ever think just because he had money, that he would spend it on her? Will she live in a house with him and freeze in the winter, because he doesn't want to pay heating bills or he shuts all the lights every time he leaves the room? Maybe he has a lot of money because he is still holding on to it from his christening, Holy Communion and confirmation. Along with his money came his control over it. He chose where they would spend their vacations, what they would do, where they would eat and the people they would associate with. She paid a dear price by being told what to wear, what to spend money on and where she could spend it. By the time the relationship was over she was much happier living on less money and being far away from him.

Is it worth the sacrifice of self-dignity to remain in a relationship because of money, security or fame? Not to me. I knew someone who slept with an attorney, hence, he helped her with her divorce.

Her attorney fees were slim to none. When the divorce was finalized, so was her relationship with the attorney. She now needed to maintain her home that she acquired after the divorce, so she slept with a landscaper. Lastly, she incurred a lot of car problems and did not have a clue about cars. Enter the handsome mechanic. This girl was good. Some people simply do not have morals or scruples. I am sure she would not have wanted to be used the way she used others.

In my story, the princess saved herself. Now she lives in her own castle, making her own money, and takes care of her own self. The end.

~

It seems to me that years ago relationships were not as hard to keep together as they are today. I was very fortunate to have three of my grandparents in my life for a very long time. My dad's father passed away at a very young age (I was only four) and he left my grandma a widow for many years. My grandfather was able to hold my brother when he was born before he passed away. My grandma was very active in the senior center and loved to dance. Anytime there was a family function, there was Grandma dancing the cha cha. At the senior center they separated the lines by age for the lunches and dinners and she got on the line of the people in their seventies. She was in her eighties, but did not want anyone to know. Grandma enjoyed ceramic classes at the senior center and she loved to paint freehand. She loved to tell my cousins and me stories which were a little scary but we enjoyed them. It was funny how my grandparents didn't remember what they ate the night before but remembered all their childhood stories, whether they were true or not I loved them just the same. Grandma never drove, so she walked everywhere. Luckily, where she lived she could walk to all the stores. She seemed content being with her friends, dragging my aunt along, and baking around the holidays, making anisette cookies and strufflers (little fried dough balls with sprinkles and honey). She taught me how to make them but unfortunately, I never seemed to have the time.

Occasionally, we would catch Grandma having a cigarette, her one little vice that she tried to hide from everyone. I don't think she ever really cared to meet someone after my grandfather died. Grandma was alone for many years and was in her nineties when she died. I am told my grandfather was a wonderful man, whom I guess she figured she could never replace. My aunt told me there was a man at the senior center that liked my grandmother, but she was not interested. She did say that she liked the attention. I guess this is what they mean when they say as people age they get "set in their ways," and she was content with her life as she knew it.

My mother's mom was a little different. This makes me realize why I grew up being such a hopeless romantic. She was adopted at the age of thirteen and learned many things in her childhood at the girls group home. She could crochet and cook just about anything. After I had my daughters, my grandmother crocheted numerous blankets, pillows, sweaters, and dolls clothes for them. Grandma taught me to crochet. It was very relaxing and therapeutic. She married my grandfather at age fifteen and was pregnant with her first child at sixteen. That was the age they married back then. She told me in Italy when you married you had to put the sheets on the clothesline from your first married night to prove you were a virgin to the whole frigging neighborhood. Imagine! How disgusting!

When they first got married they lived downstairs in her mother's house. After a fight with Grandpa one night, she ran upstairs and told her mother. Her mother told her "you made your bed, now you have to lie in it." Certainly not what mothers of today would advise their daughters. Grandpa loved his Chianti red wine and gallon jugs were always on the table. He grew his own peaches in his yard and loved to soak them in the red wine. Grandpa also loved his German Shepherd dogs Fluffy, and Duchess. He used to yell in Italian and English, telling the dogs to go pee. I think German Shepherds are one of the smartest dogs. I really believe Fluffy understood my brother was small; he was three and a half years old. Whenever my brother would go up or down the concrete stairs on the outdoor porch, wherever that dog was, he would run to my brother's side to guide him so he wouldn't fall. My grandfather enjoyed going to the racetrack and fishing. He was in the newspaper for catching the biggest striped bass, on record, on Long Island and my grandmother was an avid bingo player. Grandma told me that when my mom was seven she had rheumatic fever and was put in a home for a year under doctor's orders. There was no cure for that in those days. She was not able to jump rope, roller-skate, or ride a bike because she could not exert herself in any way, until she was better. Grandma's mission in life was to take care of my grandfather and raise her children. My grandfather would bring his gallon of Chianti wine to the table and my grandmother would bring dinner to the table as he sat and waited. They truly loved each other and being together. Unfortunately, she lost one of her daughters to spinal meningitis at the age of five. I happened to be playing with stuff in her drawers and stumbled upon the photo of her daughter in the coffin. Imagine, they took pictures of the dead back in those days and saved them.

My mom told me she remembered her sister begging and begging to wear this certain dress Grandma bought, but Grandma said it was for Christmas. She died Thanksgiving morning and was buried in the dress she loved so much.

My grandfather lived until he was seventy-five and developed lung cancer and was sick for a year before he died. I remember my grandmother giving him morphine shots in the leg. I wondered if I could ever do that for someone? After my grandfather died, my grandmother wanted to stay in the house they shared for a few more years. When she was ready to move, she decided she wanted to live closer to the beach, near the boardwalk. We moved her into a cute little apartment on the fifth floor.

Even Grandma has a dating story for me to share. Every day she would go down to the boardwalk and sit in the sun. One day while sitting outside, a man named Luigi sat next to her and started up a conversation. He told her he lived in the assisted living apartments across the street and had been widowed for many years. She told him she loved bingo and she took a cab a few times a week to go. He said he would love to join her, so they started going to bingo together.

She would cross the street some days and go to his apartment building that had a large porch with swings. They would sit together on the two-seater swings and talk all day. After some time, he went to her apartment and she cooked for him. She loved to cook, and her specialty was fish, and, of course, her fabulous gravy and everything that she parmigianed. When my dad went hunting he knew where to bring the deer meat. She could make sawdust taste delicious. After a great meal, Luigi would stay for coffee and he loved to watch wrestling. She knew nothing about wrestling, but sitting on the couch, holding his hand while he watched television, was good enough for her.

I don't remember my grandfather being affectionate but Luigi was. He asked his daughter one day to take him to the jewelry store because he wanted to buy my grandmother a gold bracelet. She never took it off from the day he gave it to her. Luigi would come to our house for the holidays and they were both very happy. My mom, on the other hand, was a little skeptical about this relationship. She did not want my grandmother to spend the rest of her life, taking care of Luigi if he became ill. We watched my grandmother take care of my grandfather throughout his battle with lung cancer for over a year. I also think my Mom thought Luigi was replacing her father to which we assured her that no one could every replace her father and Grandma really benefitted by his company. Before Luigi came along, Grandma called us for every little thing. After she met Luigi, we hardly heard from her. Ah, love! Unfortunately, a few years later he got very sick and passed away.

Grandma lived with me for two years after Luigi passed because she didn't want to be alone. Food shopping with her was a riot. Because she lived through the Depression, she was always afraid to run out of food. I would have two wagons full of groceries. One girl in the supermarket said, "Don't you only have two daughters?" I said, "Yeah and Grandma." She also believed in stocking up when it snowed, fearing we were never going to get out.

I miss the Friday nights when she made calzones the size of the kitchen table and flour was everywhere. We would then go to bingo at 4:30. It started at 7:00, but she had to get there early to get her boards together, which they used back then. She loved her dessert at bingo. She said she needed a little something sweet to digest. That was her reasoning for fattening treats. I remember asking her why she always took her little sweater with her. I didn't realize then that older people feel the cold more and she wasn't a fan of air conditioning. Today, I am always taking a little sweater or jacket everywhere. Grandma must be in heaven laughing.

8.

Back to the Bronx

I lived upstate for thirty-two years before making my way back to the Bronx. I have some childhood friends who moved to New Jersey and various other places but also found their way home back to the Bronx years later. I never lost my accent. After all that time away, it was like I never left. I missed having everything so close. I have my nail and hair salon around the corner along with a bakery, drugstore, dentist and numerous bars and restaurants where you can eat outside.

Now that my girls are grown and living and working in Manhattan, I had found myself wondering why was I still living in the country? Don't get me wrong, I had friends there that are like my family. I was working in the city, and I told my friends practically every day what a freak show it was in Manhattan. From upstate, I was taking the express bus that brought me into the Port Authority, which leaves a lot to be desired. There were many homeless, drugged up, drunk and mentally unstable people. I was certainly, out of my element coming from Orange County. My commute from the Bronx now has me on four trains and two buses each day, but, it was more direct and a lot cheaper.

There are many reasons why moving back to the Bronx was a great idea. My family still lives here, which was most important. The Bronx Zoo, New York Botanical Gardens, Orchard Beach, Arthur Avenue and many other nice places to visit are all so close to me now. I didn't go to the beach much when I was living, upstate. The Jersey Shore and Long Island were a bit of a hike. Pelham Bay Park has a great running track. Of course, there is Yankee Stadium and City Island that I love to visit. Who could ask for any better restaurants than you will find on Arthur Avenue, the real Little Italy! Penny Marshall lived on the Grand Concourse and, of course, Jennifer Lopez (my idol) came from, Castle Hill Avenue. Salsa and Hip-Hop were also born in the Bronx.

~

People asked me how it was for me going back after all these years. I never felt like I had to fit in the Bronx again, I was born here. In November 2015, I moved back to an adorable two-bedroom apartment, about eight minutes from my parents' house. I attend church with them on Saturday nights and we often have dinner together.

Before I moved, I got a great job in a fabric company in Manhattan. The people are just wonderful; they have been very professional and helpful from the start. I'd rather shuffle through fabric than legal documents anytime. My employer is very generous and I love donating fabric to worthy organizations. There are so many ways to empower women, even through donating fabric. The small pieces of material can go to the cancer patients for their kerchiefs. There are people that make prom gowns for girls to be able to attend their first formal party and makeover organizations to dress women to get them into the work force. One of my favorites is the women who make dresses to send to needy girls in Haiti and other countries that have never worn a pretty dress.

When I started my commuting experience, I asked a train comptroller if I was taking the correct train and he was very helpful. The next day I saw him and thought with all these people passing through, he would not remember me from yesterday, so I asked him again, just to be sure, and he said, didn't I see you yesterday and you asked me the same question? How embarrassing, but, he was so sweet. I told him many people were giving me wrong directions. Now every morning we say hello, have a good day, enjoy your weekend, whatever. If he sees me running for the train, he tells the conductor to hold the train and I mosey on in, feeling like I'm someone important.

Sometimes, it pays to talk to strangers.

The first day commuting was not fun. The train was having brake problems, so we were stuck underground for forty-five minutes without cell service. They came on the tracks to fix the brakes to no avail. We got pushed to the next stop and had to get off and switch trains. Switch trains to where? I had no idea what train to get on. I asked the girl next to me and fortunately, she was going to 34th Street, as she worked in Macys. We got on the 1 and I made it to work, an hour late. One of the most amazing things is that I can sleep on a train standing up, holding a pole over my head, swinging back and forth while the man on my left is rapping with one curse word after the other and the man on my right is playing "La Bamba" on his guitar.

One day on the train a woman got on with a baby in a stroller and two toddlers. One child was screaming and she proceeded to discipline the child by telling her to yell louder. Did she forget she was on a train at 7:15 in the morning? Everyone's faces were twitching and the other child had a tantrum and the mother said "Go ahead and throw yourself on the floor." People are moving out of the way so this kid could throw herself on the floor. I wanted to tell this woman (nut) that the train floor is probably the filthiest place you could walk on. I think the passengers wanted to applaud when she came to her stop.

Things have certainly changed since I worked for the FBI and rode the trains many years ago. Back then, the trains were covered in graffiti and they had no air conditioning. We used to ride between the cars for air. Doing that has been illegal for some time. It was a lot cheaper back then too. When getting off the train one day a man had his eyes covered with his hands and had his middle finger up in the air. Did it make him a good person if he didn't see himself giving everyone the finger? Like I said before, every day is a freak show.

I did quite a bit of dating since moving back to the Bronx. Gregory and I met at a bar. We lived close to each other, which makes dating a lot easier to grab a cup of coffee or a cocktail during the week. Speaking of cocktails, on the first date he had quite a few drinks before dinner, with dinner and after dinner. Maybe he was nervous or he drinks a lot but knows his limit. It was the same scenario for the next three dates. I met him at the restaurants, so I was not worried about driving in the car with him. He didn't stagger or slur his speech, so that was a plus. Gregory had a high alcohol tolerance. I, on the other hand have two wines and there goes that buzz. I have zero tolerance. He worked for a car dealership and always drove a different car to meet me. I guess they didn't know he had alcohol issues.

On the last date with Gregory, my car would not start, so he offered to drive me home. I figured it was a ten minute ride to my apartment, so what were the chances of something happening and I could pick up my car the next day. Well Gregory proceeded to pass the only three lights to get to my place and veered a little into the other lane.

There was no need to explain to him that I did not feel comfortable dating him anymore. My horrified face explained why. I had no words.

I was starting to wonder why the universe put so many people with addictions in my path. This was scary and certainly not one of my smartest choices. I met Ryan at a singles dance in Manhattan on a Saturday night. While my friend was chatting away with someone she met, him and I went outside to have a cigarette and talked. He had been married for only four years, had a daughter and then divorced. He seemed normal enough, (whatever that means). The next day we agreed to meet in New Jersey for lunch.

When I saw him he was shaking and sweating and took off his shirt. I knew someone who had hypoglycemia and had similar symptoms. I thought that was the issue here. I thought we'd get him a candy bar with lots of sugar and he would be fine. Unbeknownst to me, he told me he just smoked crack. According to him, he had things under control. I didn't know whether to call an ambulance or not. While speeding home, my mind went crazy wondering what if he hadn't told me he was on crack and got in my car, raped me, put drugs in my car and I got arrested with him? I couldn't get home fast enough, crying the whole way home and thanking God that situation hadn't been worse.

Sometimes we do dumb things, which is the learning process to help us grow. You can bet I have never gotten into a situation like that again.

I am happy to say that not all single dances end like mine. My friend Priscilla never wanted to go with me to singles dances or with a group of her other friends. We went once and it was a night everyone was just standing around, starring at others and no one was asking anyone to dance. Some nights are better than others. It was a funny night, though. We sat around and they had coffee and cake after the appetizers. She asked people at the table if she could bring over some coffee or cookies. I told her to sit down and enjoy herself as she was wasn't the waitress. She could not help herself and is a great hostess in her home.

One night the other girls decided not to tell her where they were going after dinner and they headed to a singles dance. She was not happy. A cute guy sat next to her and they talked and talked. Although he put his hand on her knee (she watched with a careful eye that his hand didn't move any further up), he never asked for her number. When he called her office three weeks later, she was very surprised. He remembered where she said she worked and he was lucky she was the only Priscilla that worked there. I remembered the excitement in her voice when I was on the phone with her one night while she was waiting for him to come for dinner. He also loved to cook and bake.

They dated for a while and then he moved in. Before she met him she had been planning to sell her house. There were many renovations that needed to be done, but she could not afford to do them. He happened to be extremely handy and helped her with so many things on her "to-do" list. Today they are married and living in the same house, with an addition and a garden of zucchini, tomatoes and cucumbers. I am sure Priscilla is very happy that her friends insisted on her going with them that night. Talk about being at the right place at the right time.

Not all of my dates were setups or from dating websites. This one was quite odd, even for me. I was on my way to a first birthday party for my friend's twin granddaughters. I wasn't sure if I passed the restaurant so I saw a car pulling out of a nearby development and waved him down to ask him if he knew where the restaurant was. He introduced himself as Jeremy and then asked me to put my hands up. I knew I wasn't going to be arrested but couldn't figure out why he asked me that, so I did. He was in his car and I was in mine. He told me he was looking for a wedding ring to see if I was married. He asked where my accent was from. I told him I didn't have an accent (That never worked). He asked if I was Italian and asked for my number. I told him I gave out my number plenty of times before, but this was the strangest time.

When I got to the party and told everyone about my pursuer on the way, they were laughing. "Only you!" they said. Jeremy called the next day and we spoke every day for about an hour. He wanted to get together and I was meeting some friends near where he lived. He met us for drinks and dinner, and we were all together laughing until midnight. He had a lot to say about his job and life. He left me a message the next day saying he was sorry he forgot to show me his muscular legs since they are awesome. I wanted to say that was probably why I couldn't sleep that night because I didn't see them. This guy with the hot legs also told me he has no trouble getting dates because of his beautiful, piercing, blue eyes. That man surely needed to get over himself. He never called again and no real loss there. Was he on the prowl or in a relationship? I'll never know. I think he did me a favor, I sure don't want to be in competition in the sexy leg category with my new guy friend.

All logic goes out the window when trying to figure out dating. They don't call because they don't want to or they are no longer interested. Oh, how it stings sometimes. I heard a story about a girl wanting so bad for this guy to call and she assumed he didn't because there was a big blackout in August of 2003 for about twenty-nine hours. Her friend tried to bring her to her senses saying, "The city blacked out; he didn't." If he really wanted to, he would have called her.

I once told a friend she could give a guy named Frank my number. He called a few times and we made plans to meet at a nice diner in New Jersey on a Saturday afternoon. Before meeting him, I had three outfits laid out on the bed and could not figure out what to wear. High shoes, low shoes—my bedroom looked like a department store. I got there a little early, as usual. I have a thing for punctuality. Frank didn't say he was very short. I backed up into a parking spot at the diner and saw him swinging his arm in the air so I didn't hit him. He had a long-stemmed rose in his hand for me, which was very thoughtful. He had on a baseball cap, dirty jeans, and filthy sneakers. Did plans change? Were we going to a ballgame? Now you do not have to sit at the diner with a Tuxedo on but is wearing clean clothes too much to ask? He also lacked in the savoir-faire department. Whatever went into his mouth partly landed on his shirt. I was worried about wearing a nice outfit and I don't think he showered.

He told me about some women he dated who were like serial daters. He said they would date a different guy every night or every other just to get a free meal. Did these girls have jobs? Did they not make enough money to buy food? If I would have had to wait for a date every night to eat, I would have died of starvation. You cannot blame these men when they suggest a glass of wine, a beer or coffee. It must get very expensive, if you ask me. Also, not sitting down for a full dinner works well when you do not admire the person sitting across from you at the table, or after a little conversation you want to run for the hills. He told me he once met a girl and suggested she pick the place for dinner and she had picked a four-star restaurant in a hotel in her neighborhood. To me that was very inconsiderate, whether the guy makes minimum wage or makes millions. She probably would have fainted it he asked her to go Dutch.

I bet he will never make that mistake again.

I put the rose in a vase when I got home and when my daughters saw it they said, "Oh Mom, how sweet." I asked them if either of them wanted it.

I saved the best for last, as the song goes.

I introduced myself to Paul over a dating website and told him he had a nice smile. We spoke on the phone quite a bit and seemed to have a lot in common. We were both full blooded Italians, both of us had daughters, liked to cook, enjoyed going out for nice dinners, and liked the beach and concerts. Paul saw on my dating website profile that I liked casinos. He said that he had no business ever going into casinos. Could it be a gambling issue or an alcohol issue? I would find out more about this later.

Oddly enough, the first date was on Valentine's Day/Ash Wednesday. With ashes on both of our heads, we met at my office lobby. He had a dozen roses and a huge card for me. We walked about ten blocks, holding hands to the nice Italian restaurant. We saw a young man at the next table with flowers and then a young girl came in and I stated that they were a cute couple. He said that the flowers he gave me were bigger and prettier than hers. (First red flag).

Paul had the waiter take about five pictures of us. He said he was putting one in a frame on the desk in his office. Would he tell his co-workers the photo is of a girl he went on *one* date with? (A little premature—second red flag.) We were there a few hours and I could not get a word in edgewise. He spoke endlessly about his job. After he didn't have a drink, I asked about the reason. He said he had an alcohol issue three years ago and went to meetings every morning. Kudos to him, I said. However, he said his brother has not been so successful with his own drinking issues and lived with their mother and there was always fighting going on. One time he was there in the midst of his mother and brother fighting and he got involved and his mother called the cops. He tried to solve the problem by punching the two policemen. (Third red flag.) He never did jail time as he knew someone, but had to attend anger management classes. (You will see by the end of this story that none of those classes worked for him.)

I basically became a full-fledged therapist on this date. He said that I read him so well. When I asked if he suffered from depression (it was a gut feeling I had, and it was not my first dating rodeo), he told me he was in and out of mental institutions for a few years. I couldn't tell you what shocked me more—this comment or him punching the policemen. I had to laugh because he bragged how at his age he was not on any meds like cholesterol or high blood pressure. My feelings were that he should have been on every medication known to mankind. (Fourth red flag.) I will stop with the flags now. By the end of our time together there were more flags flying than at the Olympics opening ceremony.

He suggested he would order dinner for me as he had eaten there before. I told him I could order for myself. (Was he being nice or controlling?) He did mention that his ex-wife said he was controlling. It remained to be seen. Anyway, I kind of lost my appetite through this intense therapy session. After three very long hours, he walked me to the bus stop and waited with me. We spoke when I got home and both agreed it was a nice Valentine's Day and that we had both not been out on that day in quite some time.

I went to bed contemplating if I should meet Paul on Sunday for a second date that he planned. I was thinking maybe he could redeem himself. I guess I have a high tolerance for bullshit. Was a second date going to change anything? The next day he told me to text him when I got home from work. I did. I did not see the next text that asked me to call him because he wanted to talk to me. He called when I had just gotten in the door, sweating from my train ride, hungry and the dog needing to go out. I told him this and he totally ignored what I said and proceeded to talk about his job. He then told me not to worry much longer about working in the city, because in a few months I could live with him in paradise (near the beach) and I would not have the commute any longer. I asked him if he heard anything I said at dinner the night before about how much I loved the city, the energy, and all the places that are right at your fingertips. Apparently, he did not hear a word. I was getting annoyed and asked if we could speak later. He was having his daughters over for dinner, but he kept texting me. I was feeling smothered. I told my friend that night if I went on two more dates with him, he would have been ready to get engaged.

When we texted again later on, I told him I thought we were not a good fit and that he was sweet but moving too fast. He said he didn't understand and he hoped I was not using his alcohol recovery against him, like most women do. I guess he forgot the other issues he had.

He stopped texting and I thought that was the end—over, kaput. Thank God!

About 3:00 am my phone started blowing up. Someone was vehemently texting me. I was in my sleep, so tired, but, I checked to make sure it wasn't my kids or parents. I saw his number and went back to sleep.

When I got up and checked my phone there were several messages from my first and *last* date. DAMN! DAMN! DAMN! *How could I do this to him? I go to church and I should be ashamed of myself. How could I live with myself? I sat across the table from him at dinner, with ashes on my head, but I am really Satan! I am nothing but a self-centered bitch, like all the rest of them! I am a fucking cunt! He thought I had character. He thought I was different! He was so wrong about me! I used him! He confided in me! He trusted me! I should rot in hell! The devil should tear my heart out, like I tore out his! I used his recovery against him! I had started our date by saying he had a nice smile. How could I be so cruel?* Oh. My. God. This was because I did not want to go out with him for a second time? After I closed my mouth, put my eyes back in my head, I got ready for work and never sent a reply.

About four hours later, while at work, he texted me saying how sorry he was. This was probably after his AA meeting, where they probably knocked some sense into him. Paul said it was not sober or positive behavior he portrayed. *Ya think?* He had said during our date that he used the gym as a form of therapy. I am a big fan of using the gym to blow off steam and de-stress, but the gym is certainly no substitution for a much-needed therapist. He asked if I could please forgive him. Could we go out again and he would get to know me better and explain himself. (I think I heard enough). Could I tell him where he went wrong and teach him how to be a better man? (If he doesn't know how to be a better man at the age of sixty-three, I'm not teaching him.) Paul asked if we could go to Albany to attend Joel Osteen's Ministries.

Then there were voicemails all saying the same things. When I realized his demeanor was nicer, I felt less scared. He did not have my address, but he could have found it somehow. I slept with the car keys on my nightstand in case he tried to break into my house I could set off my car alarm, which was advice from a very dear friend. My friend said this story sounded like a Lifetime movie.

I answered the last voicemail because he asked for forgiveness, which was one of the steps of his AA program. I told him I forgave him, wished him well, and to please not contact me ever again. I then blocked his number. He replied with a sad emoji face.

Needless to say, I ended my off-and-on ten-year relationship with this dating website, and deleted my account *forever!*

~

I was living in the Bronx about a year and a half when I got called for jury duty. After figuring out how the hell to get there, I got off the train onto a crowded bus where I couldn't see out of the windows. On the bus was a young man who was tattooed from head to toe and wore a bandanna, scruffy beard and pants hanging off his ass. He looked like he just committed a murder or two. He approached me with his glassy eyes and said he saw me looking around and heard me ask the bus driver for the stop for the courthouse. He said that the passenger in the wheelchair gets off the same stop and just keep an eye on him. I thanked him profusely. Wow! Never judge a book by its cover.

The greatest thing about being back in the Bronx is being back with my family and helping them when they need me. Since living in the Bronx again, my brother and I hang out together quite a bit. We love the beach, seafood, and City Island is our favorite place to go out to eat. We also argue quite a bit. He sees things so different than I do. When leaving the casino one day, we were arguing and a couple heard us and said, "See they argue a lot like we do," thinking we were married. They said they have been married for twenty years. My brother said "Married? We're not married. If we were he would have killed me by now." I said, "Married? I would have never married him in the first place!" After we all had a good laugh, I told them we were brother and sister. We both are so different. I eat a lot healthier than he does, I am always punctual and he seems to always be late.

My brother is no exception to a date turned sour.

He has also been divorced for quite awhile after an eight-year marriage. He did plenty of dating and had a lot of one-night stands.

He used to ask me why he didn't meet girls like me who had one drink and got a little buzz. The girls he was meeting could drink him under the table—and he could drink. On one particular date the girl had six cosmos, and then she ordered lobster tails. Get the bank book ready for that one.

He met a sweet little girl that unfortunately, he crossed. Apparently, he had gone to a bar in the neighborhood to be with another girl, and she followed him there. Some girls recognize "game" before you play it. When he came out to his car, he found glass all over the place. She had broken every window on the car. Ah, revenge is sweet, so they say. He should be thankful she didn't slash the tires too. I guess she wasn't that mad.

When he drove the car to the auto glass repairman the next day, the guy said "Tough Night?" You bet!

I have come full circle in my life. So many things have changed, and yet, so many things remained the same. I am so blessed to live close to my family. I have reconnected with friends from grammar school and high school.

I attend mass at the church where I received all of my sacraments, including marriage.

One day a Eucharistic minister saw me with my parents and said her family and ours lived on the same block when I was a toddler, before my parents bought the house they still live in. She used to give me haircuts.

I had a great childhood and I feel like being back in the Bronx is having me re-live my childhood all over again—and I absolutely love it!

Epilogue

In writing this book, I hope to help people always look at the bright side and try to find humor in life when it seems there is certainly nothing funny about a situation. I want people to know they are not alone with the crazy, wonderful, and funny dating experiences we all may have encountered.

It is never too late to find inner passions and to go forward to pursue them. My message is to always believe in yourself. *No one*, and I repeat *No one* will ever know what is best for you but yourself.

If you love to write, keep writing—whatever it may be about. Save everything you write and one day you may be writing a book of your own.

It would have been nice to end this book telling you that I met a great man and we lived happily ever after. I *haven't*— *yet*. Do I still believe in finding love? Absolutely! We are all the result of our experiences and memories, and I have an amazing life and am very lucky to have had amazing people all around me.

I am strong. I probably love more than I will ever get back. I know that—yet I will always love and would not want it any other way.

About the Author

Annette is an early riser and a true believer in "the early bird catches the worm." She has a great love for dogs and a great weakness for brownies, which she can eat raw, burnt, or frozen. She loves to travel, especially on cruises. She loves getting facials. She has been living back in the Bronx, where she grew up, for the past three and a half years. When living in upstate, New York, she was very active in her church, singing in the choir and teaching religious education to first graders for five years. She loves to help others and currently volunteers in a Bronx nursing home, feeding the residents and taking the ladies to the salon on Saturday mornings for their hair appointments.

She loves weddings, a good tearjerker movie, music, and laughing with her friends until they cannot breathe and their eyes are tearing. She has been dating for the past twenty-one years in the New York area.

71429218R00073

Made in the
USA
Middletown, DE